The First Lives of
Alfredo Catalani

Alfredo Catalani, c. 1880

The First Lives of
Alfredo Catalani

Alfredo Soffredini

Giuseppe Depanis

With Catalani's Letters to Stefano Stampa
And 'Catalani on Record: The 78 Era' by
Stanley Henig

Edited, annotated, and introduced by
David Chandler

Translated by Ornella Trevisan,
Richard M. Berrong & Giulia Martino

First published in this form by Durrant Publishing, 2011

Copyright © 2011 David Chandler
All rights reserved

Hardback   ISBN 978-1-905946-25-9
Paperback ISBN 978-1-905946-26-6
ePub   ISBN 978-1-905946-27-3

First Edition

∞ The paper used in this publication meets the minimum requirements of the American National Standard for Information Sciences – Permanence of Paper for Printed Library Materials, ANSI Z39.48-1992. The paper is acid-free and lignin-free.

Printed and bound by Lightning Source
Published by Durrant Publishing
82 Earlham Road, Norwich, NR2 3HA

For Kaori
Who shares a birthday with Catalani

DAVID CHANDLER is an Associate Professor in the English Department at Doshisha University, Kyoto. His published work is mostly in the field of English literature, but in addition to the present book he has also edited *Alfredo Catalani: Composer of Lucca*. His website is at: http://www.davidjchandler.co.uk/

ORNELLA TREVISAN has translated poetry and prose into Italian, and also collaborated with her husband, the poet and critic Peter Robinson, on many translations into English.

RICHARD M. BERRONG is a Professor of French literature at Kent State University, where he is the director of the Master in Liberal Studies programme. He has published in various fields, primarily on French novelist Pierre Loti, but also on Puccini. He has published an edited collection of Catalani's letters, *The Politics of Opera in Turn-of-the-Century Italy: As Seen Through the Letters of Alfredo Catalani*.

GIULIA MARTINO recently graduated from the University of Milan with a Master's degree in Languages, Cultures and International Communication. She is a former student of the Japanese Language and Culture exchange programme at Doshisha University.

STANLEY HENIG, Professor and Deputy Pro-Chancellor of Lancaster University, is Managing Director of Historic Masters Ltd, a company issuing vinyl 78rpm records directly pressed from original metals in the archives of EMI and Deutsche Grammophon, and also a Trustee of the Historic Singers Trust. He is co-author of *Enrico Caruso: Recollections and Retrospective* (Symposium Records, 1998), and has contributed various essays to the St. James *International Dictionary of Opera*.

Contents

Acknowledgements ix
List of Illustrations x

David Chandler:
Introduction: 'Genius and Illness' 1

Alfredo Soffredini: (*Translated Richard M. Berrong*)
Alfredo Catalani 27
Alfredo Catalani (Obituary) 37

Giuseppe Depanis: (*Translated Giulia Martino*)
How I Became a Wagnerian 53

Giuseppe Depanis: (*Translated Ornella Trevisan*)
Alfredo Catalani: Notes – Memories 67
Alfredo Catalani: A Later Memoir 111

Alfredo Catalani: (*Translated Richard M. Berrong*)
Letters to Stefano Stampa, 1875–1885 139

Stanley Henig:
Catalani on Record: The 78 Era 153

Acknowledgements

WE ARE grateful to the Art Gallery of Western Australia for permission to reproduce the Richard Parkes Bonington painting which appears on the cover, to Erik Bruchez, who runs mascagni.org, for generously supplying the image of Alfredo Soffredini, to Nestor Masckauchan of Tamino (operacollectors.com) for letting us publish the signed Toscanini photograph, and to the Tully Potter Collection for allowing us to reproduce the photograph of Hina Spani.

Paul Durrant has again been a terrific publisher, lavishing care on the presentation of the text.

Michael Sharp, of Cambridge University Press, took the question about Virgil's 'Greek propositions' to some of the leading authorities in the world of Classics (see pp. 28–29).

The biggest thanks, again, must go to Giulia Martino, whose role in the book has been considerably larger than the contents page might suggest. She has patiently and promptly answered dozens of questions about difficulties in the translations and made the editor's work immeasurably easier. She also took responsibility for the translated material in the introduction and managed to track down an absolutely pristine copy of Giuseppe Depanis's rare *L'Anello del Nibelungo di Riccardo Wagner*.

Stanley Henig wishes to acknowledge the generosity of numerous collectors who made it possible for him to listen to recordings, many very rare in their original form, and in some cases never transferred to LP or CD.

List of Illustrations

Alfredo Catalani, c. 1880*. . . . . **Frontispiece**

Alfredo Catalani, c. 1889. By Vespasiano Bignami[1] 26

Alfredo Soffredini (1854–1923) 33

Alfredo Catalani, c. 1891[2] 36

Roberto and Alfredo Catalani, mid-1860s[3] 43

Giuseppe Depanis, 1911[4] 52

Carlo Rossaro (1828–78)*. 57

---

1 This, the original illustration to Soffredini's 1890 article, had been published earlier as the frontispiece to *Impressioni*, the collection of Catalani's piano music Casa Ricordi brought out early in 1890. The reproduction here was scanned from the superior quality image in *Impressioni*. Bignami (1841–1929) was a well-known painter and art critic, associated, like Catalani, with the Scapigliatura.

2 This, the original illustration to Soffredini's obituary article, had been published earlier on 24 January 1892 to mark the premiere of *La Wally*. See Maria Menichini, *Alfredo Catalani alla luce di documenti inediti* (Lucca, 1993), Fig. 37.

3 Illustration from Carlo Gatti, *Catalani: La Vita e le Opere* (Milan, 1953), plate after p. 16.

4 Illustration from David Sorani, *Giuseppe Depanis e la Società di Concerti: Musica a Torino fra Ottocento e Novecento* (Turin, 1988), Fig 3.

Alfredo Catalani, *c.* 1892*..............................66

Carlo Pedrotti (1817–93)*............................73

Giovanni Depanis (1823–89)*........................110

Arturo Toscanini, 1904..............................123

Facsimile of Catalani's Letter to Depanis, 3 August 1890*....134

Stefano Stampa. Self-portrait[1]........................138

Hina Spani (1896–1969)............................152

* These illustrations are taken from the two volumes of Giuseppe Depanis, *I Concerti Popolari ed Il Teatro Regio di Torino* (Turin, 1914–15)

---

1 Illustration from Ezio Flori, *Il Figliastro del Manzoni, Stefano Stampa* (Milan, 1939), vol. I, plate after p. 208.

Introduction: 'Genius and Illness'

In 1900 Arnaldo Bonaventura (1862–1952) was asked to give a lecture by the Società Musicale Guido Monaco in Lucca, as part of their commemoration of Alfredo Catalani. Turning to his subject, Bonaventura, a distinguished musicologist and music historian, raised the question:

> Need I tell you the story of his [Catalani's] life? Surely not. You know it much better than I do, you who have lovingly followed him since his first steps, who listened to his first Mass, for four soloists and large orchestra, written for the cathedral in Lucca, and who sent him off with top marks so that he was accepted *without an exam* to the advanced composition class at the Paris Conservatoire. You who admired the conscience of the artist when, back from the French capital, enriched with knowledge, instead of putting on haughty airs ... [he] wanted to further deepen his studies, humbly setting off to Milan to follow Antonio Bazzini's teachings, and honourably earning, after a further two years of study, the final diploma and baptism as a composer with his idyll *La Falce*. You who rejoiced at the repeated triumphs of his operas,

you who were proud to see him take up the composition chair at the Milan Conservatory, succeeding the illustrious [Amilcare] Ponchielli, you, finally, who felt anxiety for him when you saw him succumb to that terrible disease that claims many young lives, that has stolen many musicians from their art before their time, and against which it finally seems that modern hygiene wants to wage a holy crusade. You who mourned, for good reason, his untimely passing.[1]

Although Bonaventura left his detailed account of the operas until later, and, for the sake of his audience, put a heightened emphasis on Catalani's early Lucca achievements, in general his statement represents a succinct overview of the composer's biography as it was understood in the years after his death. Catalani was the brilliant youth who had taken the unusual step, for an Italian composer, of studying abroad; his career had effectively started with *La Falce* (1875), which had caused a stir; he had gone on to write several more successful operas, and had obtained an important academic position, and yet his life had been blighted and finally destroyed by tuberculosis, leading him to an early grave at the age of thirty-nine.

That story was sufficiently tragic, no doubt. Yet another could have been told – and is told in the present book – of a bleaker and frustrated existence, of a marvellously gifted composer who never quite achieved his promise, of a creative life broken up by long periods of inactivity forced by illness, the need to earn money, the lack of a libretto, the long delays that preceded the production of completed operas, or any combination of these. The story of a man almost compulsively attached to the idea that he was only ever 'half lucky,' for whom every positive

---

[1] *Onoranze al maestro Alfredo Catalani* (Lucca, 1900), 95–96.

development seemed to be attended by misfortunes, who lost the support of his mentoring publisher, Giovannina Lucca, just as he had established himself as the leader of the younger Italian composers, who saw his two finest achievements rapidly eclipsed by the explosive successes of Mascagni's *Cavalleria Rusticana* and Puccini's *Manon Lescaut* respectively, and who never found happiness in love.

Nonetheless, the juxtaposition of the notions of 'genius and illness' in Bonaventura's sunnier account, to use a phrase from Giuseppe Depanis's 1893 memoir of the composer, highlights the twin poles around which any understanding of Catalani's life is bound to revolve. Some may dispute the accolade of genius, but even critics largely out of sympathy with his work have never questioned that Catalani was naturally endowed with great musical gifts and had both the ability and ambition to change the course of Italian opera. With the marvellously mature *La Falce* (1875), composed at the age of twenty to a libretto by none other than Arrigo Boito, Catalani revealed himself the most promising and progressive young composer in Italy, the one most likely to confidently lead Italian opera to a post-Verdi future. If his subsequent career did not develop as he wished, and if Catalani, in his final years, was obliged to see Mascagni and Puccini seize the imagination of the public and the place in operatic history he had dreamed of for himself, then a great share of the blame can be attributed to his illness. Tuberculosis not only prevented Catalani working for long periods, and used up his time and slender income as he travelled regularly to spas in a largely doomed search for better health, it also afflicted and frustrated most other aspects of his life. It lost him the chance of marriage, and almost lost him the chance to succeed Ponchielli as Professor of Composition at the Milan Conservatory. It turned him in on himself, made him anxious and pessimistic. And there is good reason to suppose that his frail, skeletal appearance dissuaded the powerful publisher Giulio Ricordi from making any substantial investment in his future. Catalani was, in short, a seriously ill and often embittered man.

Catalani was born a generation too early to benefit from the great advances in the medical understanding of tuberculosis that took place in the mid- and late nineteenth century, leading to the public health measures Bonaventura gestured at in his 1900 account. The knowledge of the condition that he encountered had hardly advanced on the classic description of consumption by Aretaeus in his 1st century *On the Causes and Symptoms of Chronic Diseases*. Aretaeus's list of symptoms remarkably anticipates almost every physical detail (apart from the moustache!) emphasized in contemporary descriptions of Catalani's appearance. In other words, Catalani exactly fitted the classic picture of the consumptive, or at any rate was made to fit the picture, his biographers, perhaps unconsciously, particularly registering those physical details that signalled illness. The consumptive, according to Aretaeus, had

> Voice hoarse; neck slightly bent, tender, not flexible, somewhat extended; fingers slender, but joints thick; of the bones alone the figure remains, for the fleshy parts are wasted ... Nose sharp, slender; cheeks prominent and red; eyes hollow, brilliant and glittering; swollen, pale, or livid in the countenance; the slender parts of the jaws rest on the teeth, as if smiling; otherwise of a cadaverous aspect. So also in all other respects; slender, without flesh ...[1]

In addition, the coughing, the production of sputa (in which Catalani had a rather obsessive interest), the feverishness and weakness, the proneness to common ailments, the constant

---

[1] *The Extant Works of Aretæus, The Cappadocian*, ed. and trans. by Francis Adams (London, 1856), 310–11.

anxiety: all these symptoms of consumption had been noted by Aretaeus and all were noted in Catalani.

Catalani, then, was a textbook consumptive, and he lived the life of one, attempting to avoid the summer heat in Milan by regularly heading to the lakes and mountains, taking frequent spa treatments, and seeking relief at hospitals and apothecaries' shops. He displayed, too, the classic phenomenon of the *spes phthisica*, or nervous force that led to 'a perpetual hope of recovery even in the face of devastating disease, and ... a feverish urge for accomplishment.'[1] Even at the very end of his life he appears to have been genuinely optimistic that his health would improve, that he would go on working and write more operas. Public perceptions of Catalani were strongly informed by the fact that he was known to be consumptive. At the premiere of *La Falce* the whisper went round that 'Catalani has a fever, *he's consumptive*.'[2] At that stage of his career the boldness of his music appears to have disarmed any potential criticism that his illness influenced his art. However a decade later, after the premiere of *Edmea* (1886), his gentlest and in some ways most conventional opera, the jibe began to be made that both composer and composition were consumptive: and the jibe stuck, to Catalani's anguish. This appears to have had little immediate impact on his popular standing – *Edmea* was far and away Catalani's most successful opera to date – but it facilitated the process by which he gradually came to be sidelined as a weak and ineffectual talent, supposedly lacking the virility of a Mascagni or a Puccini. '[H]is languishing body prompted the argument about the languor of the music,' Giuseppe Depanis concluded in 1915.[3]

---

[1] René and Jean Dubos, *Tuberculosis, Man, and Society*, 2nd edn. (New Brunswick and London, 1987), 59.

[2] *Alfredo Catalani: Composer of Lucca*, ed. David Chandler, 2nd edn. (Norwich, 2011), 112. Hereafter *Composer of Lucca*.

[3] See below, p. 125.

There is something of a paradox here, however, and it is one which runs through Catalani's critical reception. Even in classical times the *spes phthisica* was associated with creative inspiration and genius, and in the nineteenth century 'the general idea of consumption as a disease of genius grew ever more common in medical texts as well as in popular opinion.'[1] Tuberculosis, though one of the major killers of the time, had been greatly romanticised and become particularly associated with poetic young men of highly refined sensibility. In other words, a lot of evidence from the nineteenth century would suggest that Catalani's operas should have been the more valued precisely because he *was* consumptive. Certainly admirers of his music regularly praised its sweetness, grace, refinement and melancholy beauty: all qualities associated with consumptive artists. Despite this, though, there can be no doubt that Giuseppe Depanis and Giovanni Battista Nappi were right to conclude that on the whole Catalani's illness and the assumptions it engendered had a deleterious impact on his critical reception. This is perhaps because opera, as a genre, was not regarded as so amenable to 'consumptive' qualities as, say, lyric poetry or piano music. One might recall Wagner's dismissive reference to 'the consumptive variations of Bellini and Donizetti' on Rossini's 'voluptuous theme' – especially as Catalani was often compared to Bellini.[2] There had been earlier opera composers with tuberculosis, most importantly Giovanni Battista Pergolesi and Carl Maria von Weber, but their lively works were less easy to associate with illness, and Pergolesi, Catalani's obvious Italian precursor in this respect, wrote well before the full development of the romantic cult of consumptive genius. Perhaps Catalani's biggest problem

---

[1] Clark Lawlor, *Consumption and Literature: The Making of the Romantic Disease* (Houndmills, 2006), 120–21.

[2] *Richard Wagner's Prose Works*, trans. William Ashton Ellis, 7 vols. (London, 1892–99), 3:126.

was simply that his music was inevitably going to be compared with Verdi's: until Mascagni burst onto the scene, Verdi, over forty years his senior, was in fact Catalani's most formidable rival. Though Verdi had composed the classic operatic representation of consumption in *La Traviata*, it is hard to imagine a more thoroughly *un*consumptive music than his, and Catalani's softer, more 'feminine' and introverted style had sacrificed a certain amount of vigour in its pursuit of a new ideal of poetic expressiveness. Verdian robustness was an operatic ideal against which Catalani's operas could be easily caricatured, unjustly, as enervated and wilting.

In general, then, tuberculosis not only undermined Catalani's physical ability to work, but undermined the public impact of his work. Artistic innovation was often dismissed as weakness instead of strength. This presented a considerable challenge to biographers, not one of whom was prepared to draw on the myth of consumptive genius to argue that Catalani's music was the greater because of his illness (though there are suggestions that the melancholy of the music was the more profound because of his sufferings). On the other hand, they were all, at least until the 1950s, sympathetic to their subject and naturally unwilling to join his accusers and claim that illness had had a deleterious impact on the operas. Avoiding these positions, they tended to represent genius and illness in conflict, genius achieving some triumphant victories but finally succumbing to a remorseless foe. The fact that Catalani's own body had been against him supported, by implication, a larger argument that he was an embattled spirit whose lofty visions had struggled in an uncongenial, sometimes frankly hostile world. There can be no question that Catalani could have written more operas and more music had he been healthy; whether better operas and better music it is impossible to say, but the theme of 'what might have been' naturally pervades a lot of the writing on Catalani. This would doubtless have been true in any case, but it is raised to a high degree of poignancy by the fact that his death coincided with a period of momentous change in Italian opera. Catalani was already well into the composition of *La Wally* when *Cavalleria Rusticana* began its triumphal career. In his final three years of life he was an often tormented observer of the rise to fame of Mascagni, Leoncavallo, and Puccini. He had neither the time, nor the health, nor, it might be added, the supportive publisher to respond to their sensational operas.

* * *

The first significant biographies of Catalani were written by Alfredo Soffredini (1854–1923). There had been earlier biographical notices,[1] but the biography Soffredini published in March 1890 was much the most ambitious to that date, and the only one of substance to appear in Catalani's lifetime. It has a particular importance here in that it obviously draws on information Catalani had himself supplied, and to a considerable extent probably represents Catalani's own understanding of his life at that juncture. Moreover, Catalani was obviously in a position to refute any false information.

Soffredini, born in Livorno, studied at the famed Royal Conservatory of Music, Milan, where he probably encountered Catalani sometime between 1873 and 1875. In 1875 he returned to his hometown to found a new music school, the Istituto Musicale Livornese, renamed the Istituto Luigi Cherubini in 1879, which offered a 'comprehensive musical education, including composition and musical theory as well as instruction on a variety of instruments.'[2] The young Pietro Mascagni started taking lessons there in 1876, and continued to study with Soffredini until 1882; 'God created me, my teacher made me!' Mascagni proclaimed

---

[1] For references to earlier notices see Maria Menichini, *Alfredo Catalani alla luce di documenti inediti* (Lucca, 1993), 96–101.

[2] Alan Mallach, *Pietro Mascagni and His Operas* (Boston, 2002), 8.

in 1881.[1] It appears unlikely that any degree of intimacy was established between Soffredini and Catalani at the Conservatory, given that Soffredini includes no personal recollections from that period in his biographies, and it is fairly certain that they saw little if anything of each other between 1876 and 1886. However in 1887 Soffredini gave up his teaching position and moved to Milan to become the editor-in-chief of the *Gazzetta Musicale di Milano* published by Casa Ricordi, a position he held until 1893. He was also intent on becoming an opera composer, and specialized in children's operas, the first apparently *Il Piccolo Haydn* (1889). (Like the vast majority of opera composers he enjoyed little success in this field.) In 1901 he published a notable book-length study of Verdi, his favourite composer. By the time he was writing his 1890 biography of Catalani it is clear they had become close friends. The 1893 obituary includes the remarkable and moving statement: 'We are writing these modest words at our table, at which poor Alfredo used to sit almost every day conversing in a friendly manner.' There is no reason to doubt this, yet rather astonishing to note that Soffredini is not mentioned even once in Catalani's published letters, and hardly at all by his later biographers: a striking example of how our knowledge of his day to day life is sketchy at best.

The timing of the 1890 biography is highly significant. *Loreley* had received its premiere the previous month, and with that Catalani officially became a Ricordi composer; all his earlier operas had been brought out under the auspices of Casa Lucca, Ricordi's rival. The publication of the biography so soon afterwards in a Ricordi magazine was clearly designed to increase public interest in the composer and with that his profitability to the publisher. So, at least, Giulio Ricordi would have regarded the matter.

---

[1] David Stivender (trans. and ed.), *Mascagni: An Autobiography Compiled, Edited and Translated from Original Sources* (New York and London, 1988), 336.

Soffredini, however, appears to have regarded the biography as a genuine testament of friendship, and it is possible that most of it was in fact written earlier: he has remarkably little to say about *Loreley* and considers Catalani primarily as 'the author of *Edmea*,' to use his own expression. As Ricordi exerted a good deal of influence over what went into the *Gazzetta Musicale*, it is not difficult to imagine a situation in which Soffredini proposed to publish a biography of Catalani in 1888 or '89 but Ricordi advised him to delay its appearance until he had brought out *Loreley*. Whatever the case, the biography, though briefly noting that Catalani had been inadequately honoured, has a remarkably hopeful and upbeat character: the general impression is that the composer has a great career ahead of him. No mention is made of Catalani's illness, even though it was clearly well known in operatic circles, and Soffredini was sufficiently assured of the composer's health to joke about him sneezing 'with a certain gravity.' Looking back on this earlier biography after Catalani's death, Soffredini noted that '[o]ur good mood filled our pen with joy.'[1] In terms of proportions, the 1890 biography is most interesting for the heavy emphasis it places on Catalani's decision to become a composer against the wishes of his family. One can infer that this episode figured largely in Catalani's accounts of himself. As the late 1880s was a rather dark period for him, it is possible he was drawn to dwell on this defining moment in an attempt to find continued faith in his career choice, and perhaps simply to revive himself with thoughts of happier, more optimistic times.

Catalani died on 7 August 1893, having managed to produce only one major work subsequent to *Loreley*. Soffredini was the obvious choice to write an obituary for the *Gazzetta Musicale*, and his extended notice amounts to a second biography. It was written in a mood of deep grief, and with a painful recognition that the sunny hopes of 1890 had not been realized. The composer's

---

1 See below, p. 37.

illness, though not named, is now allowed its full power: 'Alfredo Catalani has died, from a disease that shows no pity for those, like him, who have the misfortune of having inherited it. It came back unexpectedly, after it really seemed that his recent artistic successes had put it to rest.' This truly remarkable statement, proposing a correlation between success and health and perhaps suggesting that Catalani's ill health was linked to depressive feelings, sits oddly beside the theme of doomed youth that now surfaces, as it often does in the biographies of those who die before their time. Elsewhere Soffredini recalls that on Catalani's face 'a tenacious destiny seemed already to have written the sentence that was carried out on the seventh of this month.'

The biographical information in Soffredini's obituary essentially repeats material from the earlier biography, but this is enriched by a much fuller account of Catalani's character – one of the four or five most substantial statements of what Catalani was like as a man. The composer emerges from these pages a shy, sincere, melancholy figure, genuinely kind and 'loved and esteemed by all those who came in contact with him.' A strong sense is conveyed, for the first time, of an incomplete career, of an artist with a strong sense of mission who never reached his goal: ideas that would be central to the later Catalani literature. Soffredini's obituary also contains a remarkably full account of the composer's funeral. This vouches for how much Catalani was indeed esteemed by the musical establishment, for Soffredini describes a well-attended, grand affair. These funeral honours did not fit with the later image of neglected genius that developed around Catalani, however, and by 1926 Raffaello Barbiera was recalling it, remarkably, as a 'miserable funeral … There were only a handful of us behind his [Catalani's] modest hearse.'[1]

Although Soffredini was clearly important to Catalani, and his writings on the composer are important to us, there can be little

---

1 *Composer of Lucca*, 140.

doubt that Giuseppe Depanis (1853–1942) was a closer friend and no doubt at all that it was Depanis's writings on Catalani that formed the foundation of later biography. The 1900 *Onoranze* volume in which Bonaventura's lecture was published reprinted Depanis's memoir of Catalani, not Soffredini's. And when Domenico Luigi Pardini attempted the first full biography of Catalani in the 1930s he clearly considered Depanis much his most significant precursor, even though he praised the 'affectionate and intimate' memoirs of the composer by Soffredini and Barbiera as well.[1] Pardini felt that Depanis's portrait of Catalani would always be 'the truest':

> Depanis wrote almost immediately after Catalani's death, and, because of the affection he felt for him, expressed his feelings with the sincerity inspired by that painful moment. Full to the brim with recollections and appraisal his work will always remain the truest, because it does not fail to criticize the composer's work where it was lacking, and because it reveals all the passion, the intimate being of the departed artist.[2]

In one way or another, Depanis has always been central to our understanding of Catalani. Before 1935 his 1893 memoir was simply the standard biography; for the next decade it continued to have classic status, as endorsed by Pardini; and since 1946 it has been Catalani's letters to Depanis, published by Carlo Gatti in that year, that have underpinned every account of his life, for better or worse. These letters, which Depanis himself had made

---

[1] Pardini strangely fails to mention Giovanni Battista Nappi, whose 1918 essay is of immense value and included in *Composer of Lucca*, as is Barbiera's.

[2] *Alfredo Catalani: Quaderno di Ricordi Lucchesi* (Lucca, 1935), 6–7.

extensive use of in his writings on the composer, and hoped to see published, are by far the fullest set of Catalani's correspondence to have been made public, and it is easy to agree with John W. Klein that they 'may justifiably be regarded as one of the major and most revealing documents of the two final decades of nineteenth-century Italian music.'[1] They have been translated and annotated by Richard M. Berrong. Given this situation, it is clear that the better we understand Depanis, and his relationship to Catalani, the better we will understand the composer – indeed if we don't understand the basic contours of the friendship, there is a real danger of misinterpreting the letters. For this reason I have included in the present volume Depanis's engaging account of 'How I Became a Wagnerian,' which appears to represent his most sustained piece of autobiography. His attractive, self-deprecating character shines through what is undoubtedly one of the most purely enjoyable documents of Italian Wagnerianism.

Depanis was born in Turin on 2 April 1853, making him a little over a year older than Catalani.[2] His father, Giovanni (1823–89), who would also play a significant role in Catalani's career, owned an apothecary's shop in the city, and his strong intellectual and musical interests made this a meeting place for many of Turin's artistic intelligentsia. Thus the young Depanis grew up in a stimulating cultural environment and became friends with a number of musicians, notably Stefano Tempia (1832–78), who taught him the violin, and Carlo Rossaro (1828–78), an ardent Wagnerian. Despite his love of music, however, he was intended for a career as a lawyer (as Catalani was), and after completing his classical diploma at the Regio Liceo he enrolled in the

---

[1] Review of Alberto Basso, *Il Conservatorio di Musica 'Giuseppe Verdi' di Torino*, Music and Letters 53 (1972), 198.

[2] Biographical details concerning Depanis are taken from David Sorani, *Giuseppe Depanis e la Società di Concerti: Musica a Torino fra Ottocento e Novecento* (Turin, 1988).

Faculty of Law at the University of Turin. He would later state that he 'neglected the study of the violin for the legal practice and neglected the legal practice for the study of the violin.'[1] Although Depanis completed his legal training, and was sometimes addressed by Catalani as 'Lawyer,' it appears he never actually practised law. In 1876 his life changed direction when his father embarked on a new career as manager of Turin's Teatro Regio. It seems probable that it was decided in advance that he would become his father's assistant. Confirming his professional commitment to music, he commenced a career as music critic in the *Gazzetta Piemontese*, for which he wrote for many years. The decisive year 1876 also witnessed Depanis's pilgrimage to Bayreuth with Rossaro detailed in 'How I Became a Wagnerian.' Two years later, in November 1878, this aspiring Wagnerian critic and assistant theatre manager met Catalani, who had come to Turin hoping to persuade the Teatro Regio to put on his first full-length opera, *Elda*.

That first meeting of young critic and young composer clearly made a powerful impression on Depanis, and he later published two detailed accounts of it, both included in the present volume. The two men began writing to each other almost immediately, and by 1880 Catalani was addressing Depanis as 'dearest friend.' Musically speaking, they were naturally sympathetic. Depanis was an ardent champion of Wagner, and his over-arching project in the 1880s and '90s was to teach his countrymen how to appreciate the great works of his hero. He published a slim volume on *Lohengrin* in 1888, and more substantial studies of *Die Walküre* and *Die Meistersinger* in 1891 and 1892 respectively, to mention only the major critical writings published in Catalani's lifetime. They were all, presumably, read by Catalani, who commented on the *Die Walküre* book:

---

[1] Giuseppe Depanis, *I Concerti Popolari ed Il Teatro Regio di Torino*, 2 vols. (Turin, 1914–15), 1:68.

> Nothing more artistic and, at the same time, more practical can be imagined. One learns to know Wagner, and his opera, better in your little volume of 110 pages than in certain biographies and studies with 1000 pages! Let it be said ... But truly, you know, there's no one but you for such jobs.[1]

Despite wholeheartedly championing Wagner, however, Depanis did not want Italian composers simply to write Wagnerian operas. Rather, he believed that they should learn from Wagner in their pursuit of a modern, eclectic and at the same time truly Italian style. Catalani, who as a young man, at least, was as passionate about Wagner as Depanis, very much agreed. *Elda*, perhaps the most personal of Catalani's operas, for there is some evidence that he chose the subject himself, clearly courted comparison with Wagner's *Ring*, and was clearly written by someone who knew Wagner's work well – and yet it is not particularly Wagnerian. When Depanis heard it for the first time he is likely to have sensed immediately that he was in the presence of an immensely talented composer capable of working out a meaningful synthesis of Italian tradition with the German 'music drama.' It was an unforgettable moment.

The shifting relationships between Catalani, his Italian critics, and Wagner occupy an important place in Depanis's writings on Catalani. In general he regards Catalani as broadly consistent in his artistic goals, albeit forced to compromise them to some extent in the early 1880s, and the critics as inconsistent in their principles, first condemning Catalani for being too Wagnerian and then performing a volte-face and faulting

---

1 *The Politics of Opera in Turn-of-the-Century Italy: As Seen Through the Letters of Alfredo Catalani*, trans. and ed. by Richard M. Berrong (Lampeter, 1992), 92. Hereafter Letters.

him for not being Wagnerian enough. Standing apart from this, Depanis represents himself as consistently sympathetic to what the composer was trying to do, although, as Pardini says, he did 'not fail to criticize the composer's work where it was lacking.' In his judgments he is very much at odds with Soffredini, and in a sense the differences between the two men define the larger differences that run through Catalani's critical reception. Soffredini's operatic values were strongly shaped by Verdi's great mid-period works, and he has words of high praise for *Dejanice* and especially *Edmea*. He regarded Catalani as extending rather than challenging the Verdian tradition. By contrast, Depanis, the Wagnerian, considers *Dejanice* and *Edmea* 'conventional,' and he is particularly dismissive of the latter, Catalani's 'least original opera.' He regarded Catalani as 'a renovating spirit' moving Italian opera in the direction of 'music drama' and he blames the greater conventionality of these operas on the librettos and, more importantly, the composer's need for commercial success. (The implied tension between high art and popular entertainment is simply not felt in Soffredini's biographies.) For Depanis, the central creative movement of Catalani's career is clearly from *Elda* (finished 1878, revised 1878–79) to *Loreley* (finished 1887) to *La Wally* (finished 1891). As Depanis had been instrumental in encouraging Catalani to revise *Elda* as *Loreley*, and he even contributed the basic plan for the revision,[1] this understanding of his friend's career perhaps subtly aggrandizes his own role within it: Depanis had helped rescue Catalani from the 'conventionality' of his early '80s operas.

Depanis's important role in the revision of *Elda* into *Loreley* is the strongest evidence of how much Catalani trusted his friend's judgment. Depanis also advised on changes to *Edmea* and *La*

---

[1] See *Lettere di Alfredo Catalani e Giuseppe Depanis*, ed. Carlo Gatti (Milan, 1946), 28–30.

Wally, and appears to have left his imprint on at least four of Catalani's operas (assuming that he would have made recommendations for the earlier revision of *Elda*). Catalani's letters to Depanis are full of tributes to the latter's 'fine critic's acumen,'[1] helpfulness, and general importance to the former. They are also full of requests for favours of various kinds, some of them of no mean size. In 1887, for example, Catalani's symphonic poem, *Ero e Leandro*, was going to be performed in Turin, and on 22 April he wrote to Depanis:

> I've been in bed for six days because of a new spell of blood-spitting, fortunately a light one; therefore, it's absolutely impossible for me to go to Turin. I therefore ask you to supervise the rehearsals of my piece (all this is confidential) and to prevent its performance with whatever pretext, if it is not sufficiently good. *Ero e Leandro* is a difficult piece and requires many rehearsals.[2]

Most of Depanis's letters to Catalani do not appear to have survived, so it is difficult to be sure about how he responded to rather peremptory requests like this. But the requests kept coming, and Catalani often wrote to thank Depanis, so the general impression must be that the latter was very obliging and always ready selflessly to serve his demanding friend. Read in isolation, the letters can suggest a rather exploitative relationship, and since the 1950s there has been a cottage industry of critics selectively quoting the passages that cast Catalani in the worst light. This is why it is important to read the letters alongside Depanis's memoirs of his friend, something that the present publication greatly facilitates.

---

1 Letter of 4 July 1887. Letters 42.
2 Letters 40.

Depanis's 1893 memoir contains the key statement: 'Catalani suffered intensely from a remorseless illness that strikes at the spirit through the body.'[1] The spectacle of illness and 'intense' suffering, both in mind and body, never seems far away in his account of the composer: it is hard to imagine him ever writing of Catalani as Soffredini did in 1890. Depanis emphasizes that Catalani was an embittered man, and while Soffredini's Catalani is a wholly likeable individual, Depanis's is not. Depanis tried to write with the sort of deep sincerity that he found in his subject, and hoped that a profoundly truthful portrait would prompt a profoundly sympathetic response from the reader. 'I often quote his [Catalani's] very words,' Depanis states at one point, 'because his letters mirror all that passed through his head, whether pleasant or unpleasant, whether good or bad, and I'm trying to delineate the profile of a soul.'[2] He was perhaps recalling what Catalani had written to him on 26 November 1892: 'I know that with you, at least, I can say everything that I think, everything beautiful, ugly, good, bad that passes through my head.'[3] Clearly Catalani, generally a reserved man, liked to vent his frustrations to Depanis, and Depanis willingly accepted and perhaps created for himself a role as listener and comforter. Had this relationship not been established, we would know a great deal less than we do about Catalani, though paradoxically he might be held in higher esteem. For while Depanis addressed his memoir to 'compassionate souls,' and while it seems to have achieved its stated aim of winning 'a little love for poor Alfredo,' when the letters subsequently came to be published separately they were often read without the sympathetic understanding and allowance that their addressee brought to them. The allowance was not

---

1 See below, p. 104.

2 See below, pp. 84–85.

3 Letters 122.

simply for the effects of advanced consumption. In another key passage, Depanis describes Catalani as 'ill-provided in the practical sense of life; in this he was a child with an ingenuousness only exceeded by his absentmindedness.'[1] This conclusion is certainly supported by the naïveté of some of the letters.

Central to any biography is the relationship between biographer and subject. In this case a series of implied contrasts runs through the writing: Depanis is strong, Catalani weak – note how Depanis frames his accounts of Catalani's death with descriptions of himself climbing in the Alps at just that juncture –; Depanis is practical and familiar with the ways of the world, Catalani is idealistic (an 'eternal dreamer') and otherworldly; Depanis views the whole business of opera with knowing, critical detachment, while Catalani is very emotional about it. Perhaps some of this is slightly condescending to Catalani, but it appears that these sorts of differences really did structure the friendship, and the intense affection for the deceased composer that shines through on every page makes us willingly accept Depanis's protective attitude.

Perhaps any biographer who writes about a life of illness culminating in early death is bound to reflect on the meaning, or terrifying lack of meaning, in human suffering. In 1893 it is clear that Depanis struggled to find any meaning in his friend's suffering: if it had meaning, it was merely to inspire sympathy in others – though even here it was of very questionable efficacy. By 1915, when Depanis wrote at length about Catalani again, things had changed somewhat. In the previous decade there had been an astonishing revival of interest in Catalani's operas, and Depanis could report, with obvious and deserved satisfaction, that '*Loreley* and *La Wally* have now established themselves as part of the contemporary operatic repertoire.'[2] Whereas at the time of his death

---

1 See below, p. 103.
2 See below, p. 124.

it was easy to regard Catalani as something of a sad failure, by 1915 there was good reason to think of him as a visionary composer ahead of *verismo* rather than behind. '[W]hile for many death is a synonym of oblivion,' Depanis could now state, 'for Catalani it was synonymous with resurrection' – a delayed resurrection, however.[1] There is an unmistakable hint that Catalani was a Christ-like figure, a 'man of sorrows' whose gentle visions had been scoffed at in his lifetime but abundantly vindicated after his death. Catalani, in this view, suffered *for* something: his time had not been in vain. A century later, with another Catalani revival apparently gathering momentum, the value of this unfortunate composer's work is still prompting excited rediscovery. If, as Depanis fancifully speculates, the dying Catalani could foresee the future, he may well have felt at peace, for there can be no question that he would have been consoled by the knowledge that his beautiful music had the enduring vitality that his devastated body had so conspicuously lacked.

* * *

I have called this book *The First Lives of Alfredo Catalani*, a title which refers in the first place to the pioneering biographical writings by Soffredini and Depanis. However the idea of a 'first life' is explored in other ways, too. The letters Catalani wrote to Stefano Stampa (1819–1907) in 1875 provide much the fullest portrait of the young composer that we have, and they are important, further, in what they reveal of the world of music he was intent on entering. Very little indeed is known of the first two decades of Catalani's life; Nappi's recollections start with *La Falce*, and Depanis's with Catalani's appearance in Turin in 1878. Soffredini criticized Depanis for neglecting Catalani's formative Lucca years, but his own writings on Catalani shed little light on the subject, apart from emphasizing the young

---

1 See below, p. 124.

composer's conflict with parental ambition.[1] Of later biographers, only Pardini had a particular interest in Catalani's youth, but his picture of a sickly, shy, studious boy who spent most of his time outside school in the company of his parents is frustratingly sketchy.[2] It is only with the letters to Stampa that Catalani really emerges on the historical stage as a complex, three-dimensional individual.

Catalani's friendship with Stampa was obviously important to him in the mid-1870s, though the two men had probably only known each other for a year or two. The relationship is intriguing, for there was a great difference of age and social class, yet the letters suggest that they met on terms of relative equality.

Giuseppe Stampa, later known as Stefano, was born in Milan on 23 November 1819, the son of Stefano Decio Stampa, a wealthy minor nobleman, and Teresa Borri (1799–1861).[3] His father died of tuberculosis a year later, so Stefano was brought up mainly by his mother, becoming something of a mother's boy, and raised on the assumption that he would never need to work for a living. Stefano was given lessons in music and painting, in both of which he showed some proficiency. In 1837 his mother remarried, becoming the second wife of Alessandro Manzoni

---

[1] See Soffredini's review of Depanis's 1893 memoir, *Gazzetta Musicale di Milano* 48 (1893), 591–97. Soffredini was particularly critical of Depanis for attributing only the 'first rudiments' of Catalani's musical education to Fortunato Magi: 'it is only fair that I point out to the distinguished Depanis that we cannot label as *first rudiments* those theories that pouring out of Magi's knowledgeable mind led his pupil to compose *none other than* a *Mass* in four parts for large orchestra … Catalani had already studied *advanced composition*!!' (592). Soffredini is surely right, but his comment also reflects his wider desire to root Catalani in the Italian tradition.

[2] *Composer of Lucca*, 31–33.

[3] Information about Stampa is from Natalia Ginzburg, *The Manzoni Family*, trans. Marie Evans (Manchester, 1987) and Ezio Flori, *Il Figliastro del Manzoni, Stefano Stampa* (Milan, 1939).

(1785–1873), the great poet and novelist, and she and Stefano moved to Manzoni's house in Milan. Manzoni developed 'a warm, affectionate, cheerful and entirely natural relationship' with his step-son, who now spent much of his time painting.[1] In the summers Stampa would travel, staying at various properties he had inherited from his father, especially a favourite villa at Lesa. At some point he fell in love with Elisa Cermelli, a young girl descended from a noble family who was one of his mother's servants; the relationship was discretely continued for decades before they finally married in 1887. In 1861 his mother died, leaving Stampa her fortune, and though Manzoni asked him to stay, he decided to leave a house which now seemed full of sadness, establishing instead a nomadic lifestyle of 'wandering … between Lesa, Morosolo, Toricella, and other places.'[2] Stampa appears to have been an amiable, kindly character well aware of both his limitations and privileges. In 1882 he wrote that he had grown up 'accustomed to being taken seriously by nobody,' and in the same letter described himself in the following terms:

> I am an artist; that is to say, a mediocre landscape painter who had some bent for music, some love of science, but no bent for philosophy, and still less for metaphysics, and none at all for poetry.[3]

A devoutly religious man, Stampa wrote a number of religious books, the first of which was published in 1882.

All that is known of the Catalani-Stampa friendship is contained in the letters published here. Stampa was a member of the Società del Quartetto in Milan, and Ezio Flori, who published the letters, conjectured that it was probably through the Società that the two men met, after Catalani's move to Milan in 1873. The

---

[1] Ginzburg 240.

[2] Ginzburg 320.

[3] Ginzburg 341, 342.

INTRODUCTION: 'GENIUS AND ILLNESS' 23

1875 letters suggest that Catalani regarded Stampa as something of a friendly and familiar patron who enjoyed arguing about music. The early letters hardly hint at anything deeper than that, but in the letter of 10 August, written as Catalani was planning to leave Milan for a while, there is a sudden deepening of the tone: 'No matter where I am, I will never forget you or your dear friendship, and I promise to send you news of me often … on the condition, however, that I also have news of you.'[1] The published correspondence is frustratingly incomplete, but Flori himself, who had probably seen more letters, judged that the friendship was *'enlarged … to something like a family relationship.'*[2] The broken series of letters peters out in 1885, but at that time the two men were still seeing each other regularly, and there is nothing in the letters themselves to suggest that the friendship was failing. Like Catalani's visits to Soffredini's house, this is another demonstration of how little we really know about his social world. As Stampa clearly liked to provoke Catalani about Wagner, and to stand up for Verdi, the letters are particularly valuable for their demonstration of the young Catalani's pro-Wagnerian sympathies.[3]

* * *

The book concludes by looking at another kind of 'first life': the early legacy of Catalani recordings. The golden age for Catalani in the theatre lasted from 1904 to the late 1920s: in this period *Loreley* and *La Wally* were part of the standard operatic repertoire in Italy and elsewhere, and many of the outstanding singers of the day sang Catalani roles. The recorded legacy is rich, and Stanley Henig has made a valuable pioneering attempt to assess just what there is and evaluate it. For anyone interested in early recordings of Italian opera his essay should become a standard reference work.

---

1 See below, p. 145.
2 See below, p. 147.
3 For more on this, see *Composer of Lucca*, 19–21.

Further Reading

READERS WANTING to learn more about Catalani's musical style and achievement are referred in the first place to Jay Nicolaisen's excellent chapter on the composer in his *Italian Opera in Transition, 1871–1893* (Ann Arbor, 1980). Nicolaisen feels that Catalani was 'an extremely intelligent composer,' and that it is a 'tragedy' that 'Catalani's music is so little known … His last opera, *La Wally*, is so masterful a work and of such obvious stylistic importance that a scholarly examination of his entire oeuvre seems long overdue.'

Readers wanting to discover more about Italian opera and its context in Catalani's period, and immediately afterwards, are recommended to look at Alan Mallach's wonderfully comprehensive *The Autumn of Italian Opera: From Verismo to Modernism, 1890–1915* (Boston, 2007).

Readers wanting to learn more about Catalani himself are advised to consult first the companion volume to this one, *Alfredo Catalani: Composer of Lucca*, which contains the first full biography of the composer by Domenico Luigi Pardini (originally published 1935) as well as invaluable memoirs by Giovanni Battista Nappi and Raffaello Barbiera, and second Richard M. Berrong's translation of the composer's letters: *The Politics of Opera in Turn-of-the-Century Italy: As Seen Through the Letters of Alfredo Catalani* (Lampeter, 1992). The letters are not very remarkable as letters, but they do include many invaluable insights into Catalani's later career (there are only two from before 1880), and to a lesser extent his personal life. Berrong's annotations are excellent.

Note on the Texts & Abbreviations

THE WRITINGS of Alfredo Soffredini, Giuseppe Depanis and Alfredo Catalani translated here are all entire and have been rendered as faithfully as possible. I have added footnotes to make them accessible to the modern reader with no specialized knowledge of Italian music, and musical culture, in the late 1800s.

Something needs to be said concerning Depanis's many quotations from Catalani's letters. These are all referenced to Richard M. Berrong's standard translation of the letters, but in most cases the reader who looks up the full letters in Berrong's volume will find the wording there rather different. In some cases this is simply because Ornella Trevisan treated Depanis's writings as homogeneous texts, and made her own translations of quoted passages. In others it is because Depanis himself misquotes the letters, usually preserving the general sense but sometimes altering grammar, omitting details, pulling together statements from separate letters, and so on. I have chosen to comment on differences only where Depanis significantly misrepresents or alters Catalani's sense. In other cases, the reader determined to know from whence differences derive will need to consult the original Italian texts.

The following abbreviations have been used in the notes:

Composer of Lucca. Domenico Luigi Pardini *et al*, *Alfredo Catalani: Composer of Lucca*, 2nd edn., trans. Valentina Relton, ed. David Chandler (Norwich, 2011).
Letters. *The Politics of Opera in Turn-of-the-Century Italy: As Seen Through the Letters of Alfredo Catalani*, trans. and ed. by Richard M. Berrong (Lampeter, 1992).
Nicolaisen. Jay Nicolaisen, *Italian Opera in Transition, 1871–1893* (Ann Arbor, 1980).

Alfredo Catalani, c. 1889. By Vespasiano Bignami
(Original illustration to Soffredini's article)

Alfredo Catalani

Alfredo Soffredini

[Originally published in the *Gazzetta Musicale di Milano* 45 (March 1890), 138–40.]

H E'S FROM Lucca. The land of Boccherini and all the Puccinis. The gracious city that rests on the slopes of the Tuscan Apennines, and has been devoted to the musical arts for centuries. The place where that art is nurtured with the greatest love. Perhaps – no, not perhaps – more gifted in that field than many larger cities. A city certainly the most renowned, after Bergamo, for the cult of sacred music, and indeed acting as a training ground for those bright minds who desire to give proof of their talent, and who can always be sure of finding there a truly artistic interpretation and performance of their works.

In speaking of one of its inhabitants who does Lucca honour, we need to pay homage to the modest city walls that have heard and categorized more music than those cities often called musical because they have more people who buy music ... without studying it!!

So then, Alfredo Catalani was born in Lucca on 19 June 1854. At the time I am writing he is only thirty-seven; he has already written five operas that have turned out five successes, as well as chamber music of all types,[1] and he now occupies

---

1 Soffredini categorizes Catalani's piano music and songs as chamber music. Catalani wrote very little chamber music as it is usually defined today.

the most important professorship in the most important Conservatory in Italy.¹ However, he has not even been named *cavaliere* yet,² so there is a pressing need to weave together a biography for him.

Indeed, his name augured well for him: Catalani. The art of sound and song had already recorded that fine name in golden letters. The famous singer immortalized in marble, paintings, and poems was not, however, related to the maestro: but they shared an exquisite feeling for art, and both sang its praises with tears, for the author of *Edmea* had and has as his most important characteristic an exquisite melancholy vein, and the famous mausoleum dedicated to *Angelica* in the Pisa cemetery is a triumph of sadness and sorrow.³

Alfredo Catalani's father was a musician, the distinguished student of Pacini,⁴ and one of his uncles was a fine composer, but Catalani did not study with them;⁵ Fortunato Magi, who taught at the Music School in Lucca, was already a teacher at that time.⁶ Catalani's first musical studies were done in secret, between a Greek proposition by Virgil and Euclid's *logarithms*

---

1 Catalani was appointed Professor of Composition at the Milan Conservatory on 11 April 1888.

2 *Cavaliere* was a title widely conferred in Italy, and it had been held by Catalani's predecessor at the Milan Conservatory, Amilcare Ponchielli. Puccini was made a *cavaliere* after the success of *Manon Lescaut* in 1893.

3 Angelica Catalani (1780–1849) had been a world famous Italian soprano, and is remembered as one of the great singers of her time. She retired from the stage in 1824.

4 Giovanni Pacini (1796–1867) was a popular and prolific opera composer, most famous for *Saffo* (1840).

5 According to Domenico Luigi Pardini, Catalani's father did 'privately educate' him in music (*Composer of Lucca*, 32). It is hard to believe that he would not have taught his son at least the rudiments of music.

6 Magi (1839–82), Puccini's uncle, became director of the Istituto Musicale Pacini in 1872. For a description of him see *Composer of Lucca*, 92–93.

and problems.[1] Certainly Alfredo's parents had planned a very different career for their son: they dreamed of him becoming a teacher, or a lawyer, or a doctor from the University of Pisa. As a result, they had him complete the entire programme at the public High School, in which, to tell the truth, the young man had always distinguished himself, even though he spent most of his time cultivating his preferred subject, music.[2] His nature called him to music to such an extent that at sixteen, still under cover, he was already treating the fugue, perhaps more conscientiously than the precepts of Justinian.[3]

The decisive day arrived, the day when Catalani was to have left his father, mother, relatives, friends, and the walls of Lucca to go to the land of Galileo to take his entrance exams in the great halls of the University of Pisa. Ah, those halls were Catalani's great fear: he understood the obligations and duties of serious study. He would not have gone to swell the ranks of the students with the sole purpose of having a good time, devouring the money that he would receive each month to pay his rent. He would have wanted to be one of those rare students who take full advantage of the breadth of learning, sacrificing the first excitement of youth to the pages and folio volumes of science and law.

To music, the mysterious impulse of his nature, Catalani would have had to bid an eternal farewell. He thought about it night and day before the deadline set, and almost yielded to

---

[1] An odd statement, given that Virgil did not write in Greek. It might (i) be a mistake; (ii) be a joke directed at the young Catalani's absent-mindedness; or (iii) be a rather odd way of referring to the Greek flavour of some of Virgil's poetry. The main point, of course, is that Catalani worked on his music between studies of the Classics and mathematics.

[2] Catalani attended the Liceo Ginnasio Machiavelli in Lucca until August 1871. For his results there, see *Composer of Lucca*, 32 n. 1.

[3] I.e. Roman law.

his desire to fulfil the wishes of his family. Today we would have one more mediocre barrister lost in the immense army of lawyers who, while fine and honest, do not raise their voices loud enough to catch anyone's attention, and one less fine musician, one whose name resonates proudly for his country and his art.

His nature knew how to triumph; the day came ... but Alfredo didn't go, he remained in Lucca. There was a storm in the family, but things quickly calmed down; Magi undertook to convince everyone that the young man, in not going to Pisa, had not made a *mistake (passo falso)*![1]

Having taken a deep breath, and freed himself once and for all from the threatening army of codicils and commentaries, Catalani applied himself body and soul to his preferred art, not without reflecting briefly on how much he had benefited from those early years of deep and demanding study, for it was easy for him to realize that he would turn out a composer equipped with extensive culture, an enormous benefit in the new career he had chosen.

Studying tenaciously, Catalani wrote an *Overture*[2] that was performed at the theatre in Lucca, and then he presented a *Mass* for four voices and large orchestra to the Cathedral Council, which accepted it and had it performed:[3] this proved such a success and validation of the composer's artistry that he was admitted *without an entrance exam* to the advanced composition class of the Paris Conservatoire.

He remained there until 1873, gaining knowledge, as can be easily imagined. He considered it insufficient, however, and when

---

1 This statement obviously suggests, importantly, that Catalani's musical abilities were known to Magi by 1871.

2 This appears to be the work that later scholars refer to as a *Sinfonia a Piena Orchestra*. It has been recorded.

3 The Mass was completed in the first months of 1872, and premiered in Lucca Cathedral in May: see *Composer of Lucca*, 41.

he returned to Italy, to Milan, he wanted to study *two* more years under Bazzini.¹ In 1875 he received his final diploma at the Royal Conservatory and baptism as a gifted and erudite composer with his first opera, *La Falce*.² The success was clamorous; the name of Catalani appeared immediately in all the newspapers. After a detailed examination of *La Falce* this journal offered the conclusion: *In this work of a student there are many qualities that elderly maestri too often lack: originality, courage, strength, inspiration. And there are also those qualities that, one supposes, elderly maestri usually have: erudition and a sure command of forms.*³

Before *Elda* our Catalani had written some very beautiful music, including two pieces which deserve special mention: a *Scherzo* and a *Contemplazione* for orchestra that, performed by the Orchestra of Milan at the Paris Exposition,⁴ obtained a most brilliant success and moved the French critics to the point of highly praising this music by an Italian.

Elda, to a libretto by D'Ormeville,⁵ was given in the first days of February 1880 at the Teatro Regio, Turin, with great success.⁶ Today that *Elda* has disappeared, so I won't say anything about *her*; one cannot say that she is now *Loreley*, because this latter

---

1 Antonio Bazzini (1818–1897) was Professor of Composition at the Milan Conservatory, where he also taught Puccini and Mascagni.

2 *La Falce* was Catalani's diploma piece, first performed at the Conservatory on 19 July 1875.

3 The writer was Salvatore Farina (1846–1918), a distinguished novelist.

4 The Exposition took place between May and November 1878. Catalani's pieces, performed in June, were conducted by the important composer and conductor Franco Faccio (1840–91).

5 Carlo D'Ormeville (1840–1924), a librettist and impresario who had previously written the librettos for Filippo Marchetti's once very popular *Ruy Blas* (1869) and Carlos Gomes's *Il Guarany* (1870).

6 The premiere, on 31 January, was later described at length by Depanis. See below, pp. 75–76.

work is something altogether different: only the ideas, the principal ones, are the same. But since, in a musical work, the ideas are its most important legacy, and since in *Loreley* these ideas are real jewels, one could say *l' ôr è lei, the gold* is *her!!*[1]

We need to warm things up! That's very easy; we can journey to Warsaw, where *Elda* was applauded even more than in Turin, much energetic clapping for the fine young man who brings honour both to his name and Italian art abroad.[2]

Meanwhile, fame opened the doors of the leading theatre in Europe to him, La Scala in Milan, which, faithful to its traditions, caused poor Catalani to experience unheard of anxiety. But finally every obstacle seemed to be taken care of, his opera was staged, Catalani had a triumph, there were more than twenty curtain calls, certain numbers were repeated, and all the newspapers proclaimed *Dejanice* a splendid opera. But in this bed of roses there was a thorn: the tenor Vergnet, who turned out to be downright inadequate.[3]

Despite that, the opera was given many times,[4] increasing its success and enlarging the fame of Catalani, who, however, remained discontented, because his *Dejanice* had been given in Europe's leading theatre in a less than complete performance! Imagine the success it would have been had the artist in question measured up to that very important role!

---

1 Soffredini's witty pun on *Loreley* / *l' ôr è lei* is untranslatable.

2 *Elda* was given five performances at the Imperial Theatre, Warsaw, in November 1881.

3 Edmond Vergnet (1850–1904), a leading French tenor of the day, who created the role of Admèto, the opera's hero. He lost his voice just before the first performance, and performed his part simply with gestures. See Nappi's account in *Composer of Lucca*, 119–20.

4 A false memory: *Dejanice* received just three performances. As Jay Nicolaisen comments, this was 'a more than respectable record, considering that the season was almost over, but ... not enough to establish it [*Dejanice*] in the repertory' (156).

Alfredo Soffredini (1854–1923)

Taken up by various theatres, the opera always met with the same good fortune. In Turin, indeed, in 1884, on the occasion of the National Exposition, it marked a great triumph for the very distinguished Pantaleoni.[1]

And after just a year came *Edmea*, at present the most popular of Catalani's theatrical works. Starting with its first success in Turin,[2] this gentle, sweet, inspired musical creation made the rounds of all the principal theatres in Italy and abroad, and was greeted everywhere with the same favour. The libretto for *Edmea* is by Ghislanzoni,[3] and the intelligent consider it one of the best contemporary librettos. The music is remarkably fused with it; such homogeneity is the most outstanding feature of this vital, eminently Italian opera.

Today the name of Alfredo Catalani is once again the topic of deference and praise. His *Loreley* has triumphed in Turin.[4] The highest qualities have been found in this new work of his and, above all, it displays that just balance which is the most important element in a theatrical work destined for a long life. Of *Loreley*, I will soon reveal my opinion; here I am speaking of its author, not analysing his operas.

While the Turin public is applauding him, Catalani is mulling other things. 'Ah, my friend,' he said to me not long ago, 'I have at hand a libretto that is *most* promising! ...' And he took off. I

---

[1] Romilda Pantaleoni (1847–1917), one of the great sopranos of her day, who later created the role of Desdemona in Verdi's *Otello* (1887).

[2] *Edmea* had in fact been premiered at La Scala on 27 February 1886, where it played for a very respectable eleven performances. It was repeated at Trento in May, and opened at the Teatro Carignano, Turin, on 4 November, with the young Toscanini conducting.

[3] Antonio Ghislanzoni (1824–1893), mainly remembered today as the librettist of *Aida*.

[4] *Loreley* had been premiered at the Teatro Regio, Turin, on 16 February 1890.

grabbed him by his sleeve. 'And the title?' I asked him. 'The title is ...,' but the word was lost, and I know no more than before.[1]

Catalani works and writes continuously; it's difficult to keep up with everything he's doing. You can say in addition that everything he's doing is beautiful, and to recognize that everything that he's doing is *good* you only need recall the compositions at the Royal Conservatory, in which very good students have demonstrated the excellence of their instructor, the worthy successor of the lamented Ponchielli.

I'm a friend of Catalani's, so there is no point in my boasting of his fine qualities as a man. You know that a friend is always worthy of the consideration and esteem that cement friendship. But everyone knows Catalani, and everyone loves him. Some don't like his disorderly locks of hair, but *de gustibus, etc.*[2] The jokers have said that when he speaks he *sneezes*, but since he seldom speaks, that trait is little noted. However, when he has caught a chill he sneezes with a certain gravity, but ... then he doesn't speak at all.

---

1 This is probably though not necessarily a reference to *La Wally*, with a libretto by Luigi Illica. Catalani and Illica had started work on this in autumn 1888: see *Composer of Lucca*, 126–30.

2 I.e. *de gustibus non disputandem* (one can't argue over taste).

Alfredo Catalani, c. 1891
(Original illustration to Soffredini's article)

Alfredo Catalani (Obituary)

Alfredo Soffredini

[Originally published in the *Gazzetta Musicale di Milano* 48 (August 1893), 540–42.]

BARELY THREE years ago we put Catalani's kind name at the head of a biographical study. We ended our piece indicating the certainty of a new opera by him, but playing with the curiosity of the reader did not give its title. Our good mood filled our pen with joy and, taking some pleasure in our innocent game, we closed that biography.

We write his name again today, but now it is placed after the sign of deepest mourning[1] which fills our pen with tears and grief for the task of adding our echo to the manifestations of true sorrow that the entire family of Italian music is expressing in various modes.

Alfredo Catalani has died, from a disease that shows no pity for those, like him, who have the misfortune of having inherited it. It came back unexpectedly, after it really seemed that his recent artistic successes had put it to rest.

To provide an accurate chronology, we will, in a few brief lines, go over the relevant details of the man. If our talent grants

---

[1] A thick black band separates the obituary notice from the previous article.

us the power to do so, we will, however, go more deeply into the artist who, as a result of his many individual qualities, earned for himself one of the leading places in art.

He was born in Lucca on 19 June 1854. Though naturally inclined to music, his first years of study were devoted to other things, even though his father was a musician who had studied with Pacini and one of his uncles was a composer. He was forced to follow the will of his elders and devote himself to the study of the Greek and Roman classics, with the goal of emerging as a lawyer or engineer. But between one school exercise and the next, stealing from family members his theories,[1] he gave in to his musical ideas, composing now this now that piece for voice or instruments.

Having completed his preparatory studies and arrived at the point of entering the University of Pisa, Catalani found the strength to rebel. It was a moment of struggle, but he triumphed, partly because he was supported by the distinguished Maestro Magi, who did his best to convince everyone that the young Alfredo could undoubtedly become a renowned musician, but certainly only a mediocre lawyer.

They were convinced; Catalani took a deep breath and dedicated himself completely to the art he so loved under the guidance and instruction of the learned and largely forgotten Prof. Magi.

Writing a *Mass* for four voices and large orchestra for the cathedral at Lucca, Catalani had a success so complete that it won him the privilege of being admitted *without an entrance exam* to the advanced composition class at the Conservatoire in Paris. He returned from there, enriched with the education he had received, in 1873, but he felt that he needed to deepen his education further under the instruction of Com. Bazzini in

---

1 The suggestion is that Catalani had secretly picked up his musical knowledge from his father and uncle.

Milan. After two years he received the final diploma from the Royal Conservatory and with it baptism as a learned and gifted composer, thanks to the performance of his first opera, *La Falce*, which caused a sensation.

Catalani therefore gave himself over to the theatre and, with the successes recorded in the press, wrote *Elda* (Turin, 1880), *Dejanice* (Milan, 1883), *Edmea* (Milan, 1886), *Loreley*, which is a reworking of *Elda* (Turin, 1890), and finally *La Wally* (Milan, 1891).[1]

In addition he wrote various pieces for orchestra, though these do not include the splendid *Dance of the Ondines*, which belonged to *Elda* and was then taken into *Loreley*.

Catalani also took the important position of Professor of Composition at the Royal Conservatory of Milan, in succession to Ponchielli. That he was worthy of this is clearly demonstrated by his young students, who this year gave the famous Institute many reasons to be proud.

Today all that remains of Catalani is what he achieved both in the admiration of his fellow artists and the regret of every feeling soul, and the funeral oration over his bier must pause, if only briefly, to deal with his nature as an artist, with the man beloved for his feelings, with his nobility, with the purity of his moral character, with the exquisite fineness of his soul. It must speak of the individual intimately, and the memories in the hearts of his friends who will weep for him, without needing to give these biographical details the laudatory appearance of the epitaphs encountered in suburban cemeteries.

Alfredo Catalani gave himself to music out of an instinctive impulse; he was not, however, called to it by any of those extraordinarily youthful, ingenious and impassioned manifestations from which, sooner or later, on one fine day will spring that culminating *moment* that decides the universal fame of a

---

1 *La Wally* was actually premiered in January 1892.

man.[1] His tendency towards music was modest, we might say, but constant and uninterrupted; it developed gradually, enriching itself with the treasures of science and art, by which he was driven ever forward, although firmly based in the principles of *his* nature, from which he never strayed. Perhaps death cut him off from the hope and desire of reaching *his moment*.

He felt himself to be strong in his calm, melancholy nature, and perhaps regretted that his power remained within that melancholy tranquillity; he did not paint many scenes hot with burning passion in which the goal is victory, the impetus revolution or desire. He took pleasure in the fineness of his own conceptions, and we can say that the kindness of his soul and his exquisitely delicate tact were marvellously delineated in his music.

I've said it before: few artists possessed or possess an artistic physiognomy like Catalani's. The same technical artistic *means*, of which he was the greatest craftsman, reappear in the same form on various pages in his scores. The same can be said of his orchestral colours; of his preferred timbres; of the ingenious embroidery, embellished, as if by a Carthusian monk; by the purest arrangements of various elements, not only the harmonic and the contrapuntal, but also those involving orchestration. But in all this amalgam of gentle, sad sentimentality, which was also the result of very fine and carefully considered labour, there was so much sincerity of action, so much precious individuality!

---

1 In making this statement Soffredini was very likely thinking of the contrast between Catalani and his own former pupil, Mascagni. Mascagni's '*moment*' was of course the explosive success of *Cavalleria Rusticana* in 1890, when he was just twenty-six years old, but Soffredini had been enormously impressed with Mascagni's productions even as a teenager. He wrote later: 'Every strand of his [Mascagni's] music was a continuous confirmation of his inherent genius, truly phenomenal. It was impossible to keep up with his production in those days [the early 1880s]; ... every one, I repeat, held a *promise* even greater than shown in the incredibly successful *Cavalleria*' (Alan Mallach, *Pietro Mascagni and His Operas* [Boston, 2002], 11–12).

Above all Catalani was *himself*; he revealed his natural instinct both in his great works for the theatre and in his little pieces of chamber music. His music may not have conquered the masses, but those among them who did hear it were taken by a mysterious feeling of sympathy and affection for him. In *Elda*, *Dejanice*, *Edmea*, *La Wally*, and in *Loreley* there are pages of sadness that have great aesthetic value. But it is never anguished, desperate sadness; rather, it is resigned, silent sadness that Christianity has elevated to sublime virtue.

From such a point of view, Catalani's death produces an enormous void in the field of art. The scepticism and materialism of today are no longer in harmony with the delicate vibrations of Pergolesi's harp,[1] but gentle souls are still to be found; they have experienced great emotion on hearing Catalani's music.

During the period of his artistic endeavours Catalani saw take place the vertiginous change of ideas and directions that led and still leads to the loss of so many fine talents. Nonetheless, Catalani, like Ponchielli before him, never lost sight of his own way of feeling. He never prostituted the physiognomy of his serene and spontaneous voice. I would say that he accepted the forms more than the formulas, because he never sacrificed the great values of the notes to the misery of a *verismo* that is the negation of art.[2]

---

1 A reference to Giovanni Battista Pergolesi (1710–36), probably the earliest Italian opera composer whose work was still fairly familiar in the late 1800s – though he was best known for his *Stabet Mater*.

2 Any reference to *verismo* today, in the context of opera, evokes *Cavalleria Rusticana* and the Mascagni 'school.' It is most unlikely that Soffredini intended a specific attack on his former student, however (even though he was writing for a Ricordi publication and most of the veristic composers were published by the rival firm of Sonzogno). Julian Budden points out that by the late 1870s *verismo* was already a 'vogue word' in the discussion of opera in Italy, and applied to any sort of 'realistic' tendencies in language and subject matter (*The Operas of Verdi 3: From Don Carlos to Falstaff* [New York, 1981], 280).

Such as he was, Alfredo Catalani left a name in art. His operas, especially the last two, are of our time; we feel them; with them he gave us the language of feeling. We will be grateful to him, we will owe him something. His mission, certainly incomplete, but realized intellectually, will always situate him for us among those dearest souls who saw and read with both their eyes and their hearts. Art sheds a sincere tear. This is his greatest funeral elegy, the best reward for his value as an artist.

Alfredo Catalani was a perfect gentleman, loved and esteemed by all those who came in contact with him. They do not remember him saying or doing anything unkind, and did not encounter from him, in the fulfilment of his artistic and educational ministry, the sort of harsh manners that often make a man of genius a benignly excused eccentric. As a matter of fact, his timid, almost reclusive personality sometimes caused him to remain a step behind, something that he might complain about, but always with courtesy, almost with fear.

To finish this description of his accomplishments, we will say that he wrote a lot of chamber works, and that one of his orchestral pieces, *Silenzio e contemplazione*, had a very great success in the concerts given at the Trocadero during the Paris Exposition.[1]

Death struck him while he was conceiving a new opera with which he showed himself to be very satisfied.[2] The news of his death was learned with sadness by many; we cannot say by *everyone*, regrettably, as in the field of art *affection* and *brotherhood* are the most deceitful words in the human lexicon.

We are writing these modest words at our table, at which poor Alfredo used to sit almost every day conversing in a

---

[1] The work was in fact simply called *Contemplazione* (it is named correctly in Soffredini's earlier biography); it was performed in June 1878.

[2] *Nella Selva* (*In the woods*), an opera that would have had a libretto written by Luigi Illica. See *Composer of Lucca*, 109 and n. 1.

Roberto and Alfredo Catalani, mid-1860s
Roberto died of tuberculosis on 12 October 1874, aged 22.

friendly manner. We still seem to hear his sad voice, sometimes expressing a desire to see his works better understood, always intent on expressing some doubt with regard to their popularity, sometimes happy, with a happiness that put colour in his pallid face for a moment, a face on which a tenacious destiny seemed already to have written the sentence that was carried out on the seventh of this month.

Poor Catalani, we sincerely lament your loss, and torn apart by acute sadness we send you our last goodbyes. A maestro, a friend like you, is not forgotten when lost, and when remembered the emotion reveals the legacy of affections you bequeathed us.

The press has unanimously wept over this early death with serious articles from which emerge the eminent qualities of the man and the artist. Worthy of note is the article by Pozza[1] in the *Corriere della sera*, a really beautiful article, written with the passion of an artist.

The late maestro was laid out for two days in the room where he died, surrounded by flowers and all the wreaths that had been given him in various theatres, some of which, like the last ones from Trieste, were really splendid.

A considerable number of telegrams of condolence have been sent. We have read affectionate words from Signora Giovannina Lucca,[2] from Maestros Cagnoni (for the Music School in

---

1 Giovanni Pozza (1852–1914), the theatre and music critic for the *Corriere della sera*. He was an acquaintance of Catalani and proposed the subject of *Nella Selva*, the opera Catalani was working on when he died. See Letters 132.

2 Giovannina Lucca (1814–94), a music publisher, had published Catalani's *La Falce* in 1875 and effectively mentored his career until her retirement in 1888.

Bergamo), Puccini, Samara, Luporini, and Mascheroni.[1] The Società *Guido Monaco* of Lucca sent a telegram, as did the baritone Ancona,[2] Count Franchi (the distinguished critic who writes under the name Valletta),[3] Marco Praga,[4] Signori Brizzi and Nicolai,[5] the lawyer Gemignani,[6] the Ferraris,[7]

---

[1] Antonio Cagnoni (1828–96), *maestro di cappella* of S Maria Maggiore, Bergamo, was a reasonably successful opera composer who had established his fame with *Don Bucefalo* (1847); Cagnoni's career essentially terminated as Catalani's begun, for the last of his operas to be performed in his lifetime was *Francesca di Rimini* (1878). Spyros Samara (Spyridon Samaras) (1861–1917) was a Greek composer who came to Italy in 1885; his operas *Flora Mirabilis* (1886) and *Medgé* (1888) had established him as one of Catalani's major rivals. Gaetano Luporini (1865–1948) was a former student of Catalani's; he had enjoyed some success with his first opera, *Marcella* (1891), and Catalani had come to see him as something of a rival. Edoardo Mascheroni (1852–1941) was known mainly as a conductor; he had conducted the premieres of both *Loreley* and *La Wally*, and Catalani knew him well.

[2] Mario Ancona (1860–1931), whose career had started in 1889. He created the role of Silvio in *Pagliacci* in May 1892 and in September sang Gellner in the Lucca production of *La Wally*.

[3] Giuseppe Ippolito Franchi-Verny (1848–1911), who used the pen name Ippolito Valletta (or Valetta). A minor composer, he commenced a career as a music critic in 1874 and soon became influential. He played a major role in launching Catalani's career in 1878: see below, pp. 69, 111. Soffredini describes him as an 'intimate friend' (*intimissimo*) of Catalani: see below, p. 50.

[4] Marco Praga (1862–1929), a popular playwright who became famous with *Le Vergini* (1889). He was one of the collaborators on Puccini's *Manon Lescaut* libretto.

[5] Brizzi and Nicolai were important piano manufacturers based in Florence, active *c.*1875–*c.*1918.

[6] Probably Davino Gemignani.

[7] Ferruccio Ferrari (1850–1930), composer, and his wife. Ferrari, from Lucca, was a contemporary of Catalani's at the Istituto Musicale Pacini, and remained a lifelong friend. He was also a friend of Puccini's. Ferrari composed in many genres of music, including opera, and was a teacher at the Istituto Pacini for many years.

Sig. Bruggisser,[1] Sig. Caselli,[2] the distinguished Turin critic and lawyer Depanis,[3] Sig. Valcarenghi,[4] the Marcello Music School in Venice,[5] the Royal Music Academy of Florence, and friends, critics, and musicians from various parts of Italy.

Those who did not send telegrams wrote moving letters, and those who did not write came in person to pay a last affectionate tribute to Catalani, taking part in his funeral.

These things took place on Wednesday morning at 9 o'clock.

Without noisy ostentation, they succeeded in being worthy of the illustrious artist.

On the hearse were displayed some positively magnificent wreaths, notably one of green leaves, of large dimensions, with an inscription embroidered in gold on rich white ribbon: *To Maestro Alfredo Catalani, mourned by his* **WALLY**, *Darclée*;[6]

---

[1] Possibly Anton Bruggisser (1835–1905), a Swiss doctor who specialized in the treatment of lung conditions. If this identification is correct, Bruggisser must have been one of Catalani's doctors.

[2] Alfredo Caselli (1865–1921), who kept a famous café in Lucca and was a friend of many artists, writers and musicians, including Catalani and Puccini. Catalani corresponded with him extensively: see *Composer of Lucca*, 71 and n. 1.

[3] Giuseppe Depanis (1853–1942), Catalani's close friend, whose writings are included in this volume.

[4] Ugo Valcarenghi, a novelist and editor active from the mid-1880s.

[5] This was the school where Catalani's former teacher, Fortunato Magi (1839–82), had been Director between 1877 and his death.

[6] Hariclea Darclée (1860–1939), a Rumanian soprano who made her debut as Marguerite in *Faust* in 1888. She created the role of Wally in *La Wally* in January 1892 and returned to the role in October when the opera was mounted in Genoa. Catalani judged that she had a 'stupendous voice' but lacked 'feeling and dramatic intelligence.' Letters 92.

another very beautiful one with the inscription: EDMEA *Ferni to Catalani*;[1] then that from Signora Giovannina Lucca, those from the Picconi family,[2] the city of Lucca, the Royal Conservatory, his friend Pietro Landi, his students, the *Artistic Family (Famiglia Artistica)*, and one in bronze, for everlasting memory, from the firm of G. Ricordi & Co. In the carriage that preceded the hearse were piled up other very beautiful wreaths, of which it is impossible to provide a detailed list.

Preceding the bier, after the Municipal Band, were the representatives of the Mutual Aid Society of the firm of Ricordi, and of the Theatrical Mutual Aid Society, with banners, and then the clergy.

On each side, all the way from the house to the church and from the latter to the cemetery, were Sig. Giulio Ricordi[3] and the Mayor of Lucca, who had arrived expressly for this, along with Count Melzi, president of the Royal Conservatory of Milan, Maestro Scontrino,[4] and some of Catalani's students, among

---

1 Virginia Ferni-Germano (1849–1934), who created the roles both of Edmea and Loreley. Catalani corresponded with her, and had the highest regard for her talents. *Edmea* was written specially for her (Letters 20), and on 23 May 1887 Catalani wrote to her 'for me, *Edmea* and Ferni are so much the same thing that often I become confused when naming them.' Letters 41.

2 Catalani's mother had been a Picconi. At the end of his life he was living with two Picconi cousins, Giovanni and Enrichetta: see *Composer of Lucca*, 82 n. 2.

3 Giulio Ricordi (1840–1912), head of the famous publishing firm that had published Catalani's work since 1888, when it bought out Giovannina Lucca's rival company. Catalani had a strained relationship with Ricordi, as many passages in his letters demonstrate, and accused him, correctly, of being far more interested in promoting Puccini's career than his own. Ricordi's prominent role at Catalani's funeral was possibly a belated attempt to make amends.

4 Antonio Scontrino (1850–1922), composer and double bass virtuoso. His first opera, *Matelda*, had been premiered in 1879, and his career closely paralleled Catalani's.

whom we noticed Mariani, Tarenghi, and Gatti,[1] very distressed, truly moved.

The *Service of Honour* was, naturally, performed by personnel from the Royal Conservatory.

Then, after the closest relatives, there followed a very numerous troop of people: artists, maestri, ladies, friends.

Citing names at random, we saw: Boito,[2] Leoncavallo,[3] Galli,[4] Mingardi,[5] Buzzi-Peccia,[6] Pinochi,[7] Villafiorita,[8] Carignani,[9]

---

[1] Eligio Mariani (dates unknown), composer, Mario Tarenghi (1870–1938), composer and teacher, and Carlo Gatti (1876–1965), later Professor at the Milan Conservatory and author of biographies of Verdi and Catalani.

[2] Arrigo Boito (1842–1918), the great librettist and composer of *Mefistofele* (1868). He had known Catalani since at least 1875, when he wrote the libretto of *La Falce*, and he later recommended the subject of *La Wally*: see *Composer of Lucca*, 126–30.

[3] Ruggiero Leoncavallo (1857–1919), newly famous as the composer of *Pagliacci* (1892). The extent of his acquaintance with Catalani is mysterious, but Konrad Dryden has recently published a fascinating photograph of the two composers playing cards together in the early 1880s (*Leoncavallo: Life and Works* [Lanham, MD, 2007], inserted plates after p. 168).

[4] Amintore Galli (1845–1919), minor composer, teacher, and journalist; he became Professor of Counterpoint and Musical Aesthetics at the Milan Conservatory in 1873, and it seems probable that he became acquainted with Catalani around that time.

[5] Vittorio Mingardi (1860–1918), conductor and opera director.

[6] Arturo Buzzi-Peccia (1854?–1943), song composer and singing instructor.

[7] Perhaps Enrico Pinochi, a minor composer and arranger from Lucca. By the 1870s he was teaching in Forlì: see Luigi Nerici, *Storia della Musica in Lucca* (Lucca, 1879), 304.

[8] Giuseppe Burgio di Villafiorita (1845–1902), composer.

[9] Carlo Carignani (1857–1919), conductor, singing teacher, and minor composer from Lucca, mainly remembered as the friend of Puccini who prepared the latter's vocal scores. He seems to have known Catalani well, and is cited as a key source of information in Rinaldo Cortopassi's rather unreliable biography, *In Dramma di Alfredo Catalani* (Florence, 1954).

representing the Società *Guido Monaco* of Lucca, Spetrino,[1] Ronzi,[2] Orsi,[3] Rampazzini,[4] Andreoli,[5] Giacosa,[6] Illica,[7] *etc.*, as well as a great number of poets and artists, among them Signora Stolz,[8] Signora Mori,[9] Oxilla,[10] Durot,[11] Lombardi,[12] *etc.*

---

1 Francesco Spetrino (1857–1948), minor composer and distinguished conductor; he knew Catalani by 1889 (Letters 67).

2 Pollione Ronzi (before 1834–after 1912), tenor, opera composer and singing teacher.

3 Romeo Orsi (1843–1918), distinguished clarinetist and teacher at the Milan Conservatory.

4 Giovanni Rampazzini (1835–1902), distinguished violinist and teacher at the Milan Conservatory.

5 Carlo Andreoli (1840–1908), a distinguished pianist, conductor and minor composer who had been a student at the Milan Conservatory and was appointed teacher of piano there in 1875. Andreoli taught Catalani, and their connection continued after the latter's graduation: see *Composer of Lucca*, 113.

6 Giuseppe Giacosa (1847–1906), an important playwright who helped write several of Puccini's librettos. He seems to have been well known to Catalani, and he had a hand in the revision of the *Loreley* libretto.

7 Luigi Illica (1857–1919), librettist, playwright and close friend of Catalani's. He wrote the libretto for *La Wally* and was working on a second opera (*Nella Selva*) with Catalani when the composer died. Illica was with Catalani in his final days: see *Composer of Lucca*, 81–82.

8 Teresa Stolz (1834–1902), a Bohemian soprano, characterized in the *New Grove Dictionary of Opera* as 'the Verdian dramatic soprano par excellence.' She had retired from the stage in 1877.

9 Possibly Gosselin Mori, a French contralto.

10 José Oxilia (1861–1919), a Uruguayan tenor particularly associated with the role of Verdi's Otello.

11 Eugenio (Eugène) Durot (d. 1908), a French tenor whose career had started in the 1880s. He created the role of Walter in *Loreley*.

12 Vincenzo Lombardi (1856–1914), conductor and singing teacher.

Com. Ricordi had received a telegram charging him to represent Maestri Mascheroni, Puccini, and Luporini, as well as the lawyer Depanis of Turin.

From Lucca, besides the Mayor, Com. Enrico Del Carlo,[1] there had also come Prof. Ferruccio Ferrari of the Istituto Pacini and from Turin Count Franchi-Verney, an intimate friend of the deceased.

At the cemetery the Mayor of Lucca, moved to tears, bid farewell to Catalani in the name of his city, recalling with moving words the great success of *La Wally* in Lucca the previous year.[2] After this ... when one could see that among so many poets, literary people, maestri, and representatives there was a desire that someone should say a word over the grave, which covered the remains of someone who had been worth *something*, after this ... a glacial silence. The silence gave Signor Giulio Ricordi a reason to step forward and speak, in deeply moved tones because he was hardly able to hide a very justified feeling of resentment, more or less these words: *Silence is certainly the best proof of the deep feelings and sadness that surrounds you today, poor Catalani. But since I see that no one is giving you a last farewell here in the name of the city where you lived, that esteemed you and that applauded you, let it fall to me to wish you this last, sincere farewell, from the emotion of my deep sadness!*

These words had a great effect and, in the comments on their motive, they were judged to be spontaneous and more eloquent than a lot of conventional rhetorical expressions.

Don't be upset by this, dear Catalani. Before the sincerity of your art the silence of those who might have spoken really

---

[1] Enrico Del Carlo (1843–1920) was the Mayor of Lucca from 1888 to 1896, and represented the city in the Italian Parliament from 1876. He had been a strong supporter of Catalani: see *Composer of Lucca*, 76–78.

[2] The production had in fact been controversial, and had made a loss: see *Composer of Lucca*, 75–76, 94–95.

is golden; your exhausted body descended into the tomb, free from those stereotypical praises that come quickly to the lips of the slightly learned when anyone passes away. For them such words constitute a final *farewell*; after such a funeral elegy nothing remains. You, instead, will remain in the minds and hearts of every honest man. The great family of art greets you, and even as, slowly but surely, the day of your death moves into the distant past, it will place your name among those that your country held dear and recalled with proud satisfaction.

Giuseppe Depanis, 1911

How I Became a Wagnerian

Giuseppe Depanis

[Originally published as a chapter in the book *L'Anello del Nibelungo di Riccardo Wagner* (1896), pp. 7–19.]

YOU WANT to know how I became a Wagnerian? Here I am to grant your wish.

I am going back many years to search my box of memories. Today is evocative. A leaden sky, a misty landscape, a pale light on my desk filtered through the window looking over the garden, large leaves fluttering in the heavy air, without the slightest gust of wind, and slowly falling to the ground: thus fade progressively the illusions of youth. Not a sound, not a commotion, nothing. The deep quiet of dead things.

How I became a Wagnerian? Dear God! I started becoming one through a combination of influence and bravado, as happens with most things in life. Carlo Rossaro,[1] one of the most artistic souls I've ever met, used to be associated with my father, and his impassioned, imaginative conversation, and the strength of his faith, impressed me. Rossaro was a fervent

---

[1] Depanis has a note here: 'Born in Crescentino 20 November 1828, died in Turin 7 February 1878.' Rossaro was a gifted pianist and minor composer and a close friend of the Depanis family. Depanis includes a biography of him in his *I Concerti Popolari ed il Teatro Regio di Torino* 1 (1914), 225–39.

Wagnerian, and though myself almost wholly ignorant of Wagner's operas I took up the duty of spreading the Wagnerian gospel on his account, and in reaction to the crusade for national art undertaken by people almost as ignorant as me. Oh! the odd struggles in high school classrooms and under the university arcades, struggles in which, in the name of doctrines and artistic trends we were ignorant of, we quarrelled just for the sake of it, for the love of paradox, for the secret desire to pass as 'grand' men. Only later did I realize that 'grand' men do not behave so, and I missed those struggles, pointless but innocent. Friends and professors enjoyed teasing and mocking me: a supposed choir of dogs in *Tannhaüser* embittered my life for a long year between a Greek radical and a Latin participle. I felt as if those dogs were at my heels.

My true initiation came in 1876. *Der Ring des Nibelungen* was being rehearsed in Bayreuth, and Rossaro entertained the idea of going to see it. He suggested I accompany him. As you can imagine, I agreed immediately!

Little was known in Italy – and not only in Italy – of the theatre at Bayreuth, and the so-called preeminent people, the generous critics who had yet to accept *Lohengrin*, thought the expedition crazy. We decided to write to Wagner himself for advice, and he was courteous enough to reply, thanking us for asking him since the things the press was saying were untrue and aimed at harming his work. When Wagner was alive, the press and the critics, especially the press and critics in Germany, never let slip an opportunity to annoy the Maestro and try to hinder him; after he died, the trumpets were sounded and there was a great chorus of hymns deifying the great artist who had previously been insulted and praising the masterpieces formerly held up to public derision. The arrival of Wagner's letter was a huge event for us: the Bayreuth stamp and the handwriting recognized from a facsimile reproduced in an illustrated magazine were unmistakable signs of its origin. We hardly dared open the envelope for fear of tearing it. And how intensely we considered those few lines that seemed to us the very height of condescension, how we discussed them! how we gazed upon them! It was very childish, I admit, but remembering that childishness makes my eyes misty even now.[1]

We could not watch the first cycle, and the general rehearsals were originally reserved to the King of Bavaria, so we were left with the general ante-rehearsals on the last days of July. The rehearsal of *Das Rheingold* was planned for four in the afternoon on the 29th. Due to a postal mishap, we only received the tickets on the morning of the 27th. Addressed to San Francesco da Paola street, Turin, they had crossed the ocean and returned to Europe via San Francisco; apparently San Francesco da Paola was mistaken for San Francisco in California.

We packed our bags in all haste and departed the same evening. It was a most strange and fascinating journey. We reached Munich on the afternoon of the 28th, too late to continue to Bayreuth. Even though he had been to Germany once before, with Luzzi in 1865,[2] Rossaro did not speak a word of German, and neither did I. At the tavern we tried speaking French: the waitress, believing we were French, frowned at us: perhaps she had lost her lover in the Franco-Prussian war. Another patron kindly informed her that we were Italians, and immediately Rossaro started talking to him, and of course questioned him about *Der Ring*: no other topic under the sky existed for Rossaro. The good German was clearly not enthusiastic, and made vague, general replies. The citizens of Munich were not exactly well-disposed toward the theatre at Bayreuth for economic reasons, and because of old disputes with Wagner; not to mention that the blond man we

---

1 Depanis included a facsimile of the letter from Wagner, dated 14 February 1876, in the first volume of his later *I Concerti Popolari ed il Teatro Regio di Torino* (fold-out plate after p. 136).

2 Luigi Luzzi (1828–76), a composer.

were talking to seemed to much prefer his foaming mug of beer to all the trilogies and all the music of the past, present and future. When he learned that we had come all the way from Italy especially for *Der Ring* his eyes popped out of their sockets and he looked at us as if we were rare beasts indeed; he drained his mug and, God forgive him, smiled at us more indulgently than admiringly. If God forgave his smile, Rossaro certainly didn't; he was close to collapsing from sheer outrage.

We took the first train for Bayreuth in the morning. Some very anxious hours followed. Due to a delay, we were in danger of missing a connection, so the intermediate stops were significantly reduced: but that meant we could get nothing to eat. We had left Munich with empty stomachs, meaning to eat on the way. Eating! Ironically we had to bless that fast: having time to eat would have meant an increased delay. At four in the afternoon the theatre doors would inevitably close: those inside would be inside, and goodbye to any left outside. *Das Rheingold* does not have breaks, meaning that if you were five minutes late you would not hear a single note. Just thinking about it, Rossaro was agitated enough to explode.

In our misadventure the sky was merciful. We reached Bayreuth around three; with the clock ticking away, we just had time to check into our rooms, deposit our bags, and run to the theatre. Nibble a piece of bread? Swallow a glass of water? Are you joking? There were no more carriages to be hired even for a wagonload of gold – and we would not have paid so much money, anyway. On the road to the theatre, a good fifteen minutes from the city, there was not the slightest shadow; the recently-planted, shrivelled trees were living on hope, and hope does not provide shadow. The July sun pierced us with its rays, waves of heat sprang from the soil, and we climbed our artistic Calvary running, puffing, panting, and grumbling. We reached the theatre as the city bells sounded four o'clock. Rossaro grabbed my arm for the emotion. We rushed into a dimly-lit hall, climbed a steep

Carlo Rossaro (1828–78)

little staircase, and heard the outside door behind us closing. Inside the gallery we collided with a couple of other people and were still on our feet when the lights went out and the first long notes, quiet and mysterious, of the introduction to *Das Rheingold* sounded from the orchestra like the gurgling of waves and spread through the deep darkness of the hall.

I already knew some short passages of *Der Ring*, together with the illustration included by Schuré in his *Musical Drama* which served as our *vade mecum* for the libretto:[1] but the initiation was abrupt, almost without a novitiate. I was like a boy pushed into water so as to learn how to swim. The first impression was one of surprise: I was transported into a new world, and a swarm of new sensations entered my soul. I was astonished. It was then that the spell was cast. I was conquered, and became a conscious Wagnerian, tenacious and ardent. I reproduce here in all its naïve completeness what I expressed in a letter addressed to my father: 'Instead of melody as we understand it, Wagner has created another: continuous phrases, continuous thoughts occurring, developing, interweaving in an astonishing way. It is music that seizes you, whether willing or not, and it makes the eye turn and the ear stretch to the stage. Every gesture and movement of the characters is precisely indicated by the orchestra, and almost imposed. In the orchestra there is a fusion of all the instruments that is new and unique: an extraordinary effect that certainly no one has been able to achieve as Wagner has.'

These few lines represent my first Wagnerian criticism. My father received the letter, absolutely not meant for publication, in the changing rooms of the Teatro Regio while in the company of the lawyer Cerri, his co-director, and dear friend Valletta, the musical editor of the *Gazzetta del Popolo*.[2] Cerri and

---

1 *Le drame musical. Richard Wagner, son oeuvre et son idée* (1875) by Édouard Schuré (1841–1929).

2 For Valletta see above, p. 45 n. 3.

Valletta copied a few sentences – a brief correspondence about the rehearsals of *Der Ring* – which appeared in Valletta's paper the following day and was later republished by various Italian newspapers. However it was supposed that the author was Rossaro, whose departure for Bayreuth had been announced; it was attributed to him by Filippi among others in his 'Second Journey in the Regions of the Future' (*Secondo viaggio nelle regioni dell'avvenire*).[1] Rossaro had reason to be pained by the misunderstanding, not me.

To make amends, it is only fair that I quote a letter – an authentic one by Carlo Rossaro – on the same topic: 'The tickets cost three hundred lire. But I never made nor will ever make a more satisfactory purchase, and were I to be offered three hundred millions to not hear the other parts of the tetrology I would refuse. After this I can desire nothing more, for my dream has been realized. I consider those who were unable to make this journey very unfortunate. I'm called too enthusiastic, so be it! But I witnessed an impossible feat, impossible! wonderful! … Only a divine poet could describe what is great and sublime in this opera. The first act of *Das Rheingold* especially, the one set beneath the Rhine, completely defies explanation, nor can it be comprehended how a mortal could conceive of the idea. This is something supernatural. The orchestra is a mix of mysterious sounds that, starting deep, approach little by little and finally pour down on your head, a huge avalanche destroying forests and bringing down massive rocks from the mountains; your heart skips a beat, your breath shortens; frightened, you try to flee: then delicate, impassioned notes have you crying, quivering, delirious. What an achievement! what indescribable ideas!' Poor Rossaro, his whole soul, his whole artistic passion

---

1 Filippo Filippi (1830–87) was the music critic of the Milan newspaper, *La Perseveranza*, where this article was published in 1876. Filippi was an early champion of Catalani's work.

was in these statements, gushing from his heart in the flood of his enthusiasm.

Each pleasure must be atoned for, and we atoned for the exquisite pleasure of *Das Rheingold*. In the chaos of our arrival and subsequent rush to the theatre we had lost the slip of paper with the address of our inn, and we could recall neither the name of the proprietor nor the name of the street: an absurdity. After running up and down the empty streets, we finally found the building thanks to a policeman. We were exhausted, it was late at night, and we hoped for some rest. Never had hope proved more deceptive. Oh! the torture provided by the beds of Bayreuth with their feather mattresses, and feather sheets, and feather pillows! You sunk down between two mountains of feathers, and the feather sheets, mattress and pillows got stuck to your skin and you sweated, oh! how you sweated, beds, people, sheets, pillows, mattress, feathers all together. There was no way to resist. We sprang out of bed, in our underpants, and paced up and down the room alternating hymns to Wagner with anathemas to the beds. Tired of the pacing, the praising and the cursing we sank down again into the feathers only to start once more a few minutes later.

We were two bizarre travellers, timid, dazed, awkward, chicks caught in oakum and unable to disentangle ourselves. On the days of the rehearsals we ate in the theatre restaurant, but on the other days the matter became complicated and the question of where to eat became serious; getting to the theatre was quite a journey. In '76 it seemed as if the townspeople were purposefully making life difficult for foreigners. Either they did not believe in the theatre, or they wanted to take advantage of the temporary rise in the price of provisions: the point is they thought nothing of future potential but only of immediate profit, treating guests as if they had gone there simply to have a bad time and wanted to pay well for it. Nowadays things have changed in part, and Bayreuth has been remodernized. The people there have come to understand that the theatre can be a source of income and that they could not satisfy the needs of thousands of travellers with the means and structure of a small town used to counting travellers in tens, rather than in hundreds or thousands. The purists bemoan the novelties which have altered the character of Bayreuth and given it the image of a seaside town. They are partially right, but these people were not there in '76, and if they were, they were luckier than us. Otherwise they would not talk about the good old days. One day we tried our luck, to no avail, three times. We were driven away from one tavern by the nauseating smell of sweat, tobacco, ale and God knows what. In a second we found ourselves seated at a table of vegetarians and escaped after the third serving of rancid spinach. In a third tavern it was necessary to fight tooth and nail to grab the flying food and drinks, for the cannibals there regarded other customers as their enemies, and fought over purloined fillets and legs of roasted meat; after half an hour we had obtained only a spoon and empty cup. Our honour was safe, and our appetite unbroken, as we admitted defeat. That day our lunch comprised a mug of chocolate and a slice of cherry bread.

Art kept us going, and we ended up laughing at our misfortunes – with mouths more or less dry and stomachs more or less empty. Our enthusiasm reached its peak with *Siegfried*.

To *Siegfried* is connected a pleasant story.

The upper gallery, where spectators allowed to watch the rehearsals were seated, was suffocatingly hot. The stalls were almost deserted, with just a few artists and masters: enough to emphasize the grievous difference between the privileged in the stalls and the poor chaps in the gallery. We had spoken of this in considerable detail with a man who frequented Wagner's house, not remotely supposing that the expression of our desires would reach the Maestro's ears. However, just as *Siegfried* was about to begin, an employee of the theatre approached us, asked if we were the two Italians, and then announced that we were allowed to watch the rehearsal from the stalls on Wagner's express orders. It was a miracle that Rossaro did not embrace the courteous employee; perhaps he was stopped by the sounds announcing the start of the performance.

It thus became necessary to extend our thanks to Wagner. If we did not want to disturb him by requesting a formal audience, it would have been easy enough to approach him during breaks between rehearsals. Wagner was constantly moving around. In his light coloured slacks and tobacco jacket from afar he looked like a country bailiff – close up, the image was completely different, the man of genius shone out, and indomitable energy and strength were reflected in his shining eyes and high forehead. Short, and a little plump, he came and went with short, quick, nervous steps; he frequently climbed up onto the stage to correct the tiniest detail, giving advice to the artists on gestures and voice inflexion, urging on latecomers – during *Götterdämmerung*, to laughter from colleagues and audience alike, he pushed onstage a performer still in her undergarments because she had not managed to change on time; – then suddenly his shrill voice would scream: *alt!* The orchestra pit would fall into a religious silence as Wagner began speaking rapidly and firmly, sometimes enriching his speech with jokes that made the professors laugh and applaud; then the rehearsal continued, and just like magic Wagner was already sitting down, the spectator of his own spectacle. Abbot Liszt, his tall figure dressed in a long black coat, grey, shoulder-length hair framing his leonine face, stood near him, solemn and dignified; slightly further away a group of admirers and pupils quietly watched and adored.

Rossaro was not at all interested in being introduced to Wagner. He did not want, he said, to be mistaken for one of those pestering people who gravitate to famous figures for the empty glory of being near them; moreover, he did not want to risk having altered, by any inappropriate gesture or misspoken word, his supremely noble idea of Wagner the artist: for him, Wagner was not a man, he was a supernatural Entity. In addition, Rossaro's extraordinary shyness contributed to his reluctance to face an introduction.

The idea of an introduction being rejected, writing was the only option. The writing and delivery of the letter were particularly laborious.

The letter commenced with this sentence – I do not recall the continuation, but the beginning was: – 'Divine creator of more than divine art… .' I pointed out that the word 'divine' occurred twice in the same sentence, with excessive emphasis. 'No,' exclaimed Rossaro, 'this is a lawyer's objection; if there was a way to introduce the word into the sentence twenty times, with all the emphasis available in the universe, I would do it, and even then it would not be enough.' I said nothing more, for he was able to enforce his threat.

The letter written, it had to be delivered; this was another serious business, since Rossaro was very keen on delivering it himself.

Villa Wahnfried, Wagner's residence, was located at the eastern extremity of Bayreuth's main street, then called Rennweg, but now named after the Maestro. You access it through a rectangular garden surrounded by a myrtle hedge. At the back is the two-storied house; in front a bust of Louis II of Bavaria stands in the middle of a flowerbed.

We paced up and down in front of the open gate. Rossaro was unable to find the perfect moment to enter. 'What if we bump into Wagner?' he mumbled, opening his eyes wide, full of doubts and hesitancy. He was about to step through the gate when he heard someone walking on the gravel path in the garden. Rather upset, he retreated: 'We'll go and admire the panorama of the countryside. We'll come back later.' We took a narrow street framed by two tall bushes of elder. We sat down on the bank of a creek. A lark sang in the sky, a strong smell emanated from the blossoming elders. There was not even a hint of a panorama, just a solitary corner of nature, all green, all in bloom, all quiet as if we were miles away from the city.

After a long wait, we returned to Villa Wahnfried. This time Rossaro quickly crossed the garden and reached the steps of the porch. A servant in white tie and tails came out. Rossaro thrust the letter into his hands and escaped before the befuddled servant could utter a word.

Thus the thank you letter was personally delivered to Wagner.

Twenty years have passed, and in twenty years how many deaths, how many ruins! ...

Today was sad, the sky leaden, the countryside foggy. But then around dusk a ray of sunshine broke through the clouds and like magic the coppery yellows of the woods were illuminated and nature smiled, a feast of colours. I thought for a moment I could hear the lark singing in the sky and smell the blooming elder …

Night has fallen, a milky moonlit night. The forms of things soften in a pool of mystery. Bells ring from the hilltops and valley bottoms: a diffused sound, sometimes quietening like a feeble lament, sometimes rising and swelling like an immense voice imploring mercy. It is the night of All Saints. In rural homes across the countryside the pious gather around the head of the family and recite the rosary for the dead. According to popular legend it is on this night that the souls reassume their mortal shapes and wander among us, taking an unseen part in our joys and sorrows. Slowly and silently crowds of souls march through the principal streets.

The bells toll and the music carries me like a whispered prayer, like a murmur of the rosary. I have evoked the past, called back memories, and at this sad hour appear before me my musical dead: Stefano Tempia,[1] Carlo Rossaro, Franco Faccio,[2] my father,[3] Carlo Pedrotti,[4] Alfredo Catalani and you, oh Sigismondo Rossaro, that took it upon yourself to continue your father's work and succumbed to the effort, humble and unheeded hero.[5]

I had started happily, but the smile hardened on my lips, and a lump formed in my throat. Yet in these tears there is an exquisite and incomparable sweetness, an illusion – the supreme illusion – of again drawing close to the loved ones who have left me. I have learned from them the religion of art, and to them I dedicate this book of mine, inspired by art, which is concerned with the works of a sublime artist now no more.

It is the night of All Saints – and this is my celebration of the dead.

Sassi Torinese, 1 November 1895

---

[1] Stefano Tempia (1832–78), a musician and minor composer who spent most of his career in Turin, working mainly as a music teacher. He was a friend of the Depanis family, and taught Giuseppe the violin. As a music critic for the *Gazzetta Piemontese*, Tempia published some of Depanis's earliest writings on Wagner, in the form of extracts from the letters Depanis sent from Bayreuth. He was clearly an enthusiast himself, and published a sympathetic review of *Lohengrin* in 1877. See Ute Jung, *Die Rezeption der Kunst Richard Wagners in Italien* (Regensburg, 1974), 112 n. 31.

[2] Franco Faccio (1840–91), a significant composer in the 1860s who thereafter largely abandoned composition and established himself as a leading conductor. A friend of Catalani, he conducted the premieres of *Dejanice* and *Edmea*.

[3] Giovanni Depanis (1823–89).

[4] Carlo Pedrotti (1817–93), a distinguished composer who had been the conductor at the Teatro Regio, Turin, when it was managed by Depanis's father. See below, pp. 72–74.

[5] A reference to Sigismondo's completion of his father's unfinished opera, *Cassandra*, on which Catalani commented favourably. See below, p. 97 n. 2.

Alfredo Catalani, c. 1892

Alfredo Catalani: Notes – Memories

Giuseppe Depanis

[Originally published in 1893 as a 43-page softbound pamphlet with the title *Alfredo Catalani: Appunti – Ricordi*. The text was reprinted from the *Gazzetta Letteraria*, 19 August 1893, and subsequently republished in *Onoranze al maestro Alfredo Catalani* (Lucca, 1900).]

TOWARDS SUNSET on Monday 7 August I found myself on the Théodule pass.[1] Through the cold, transparent air a pinkish light was diffused which seemed to kiss the large cone of the Breithorn, while the lower side of the glacier, in shade, became empurpled with glaucous transparencies; on a rock near the hut, a squatting girl, elbows on knees and chin on hands, was looking down and about at the amphitheatre of gigantic mountains; wherever she turned her eyes, there was nothing but sky and ice. Little by little, the sun was setting, and, with dusk, the shades reached the peaks and the pink faded, became

---

1 The Col Théodule ('Col de St. Théodule'), a high (3,317m) Alpine pass between the Matterhorn and the Breithorn. Depanis was there preparatory to climbing the Breithorn, as his later account makes clear (see below, p. 131). The ascent to the pass was relatively easy, and it became popular with the development of mountaineering in the 1800s; a hut was built there for the convenience of climbers which became known as the Pavilion du Col St. Théodule.

blue, changing into a milky grey-colour. It was a superbly melancholy spectacle, demanding admiration and insinuating into the spirit a sweet sadness, a sadness drawn from the immensity. Spontaneously, as if its artistic image had appeared, there arose in me a memory of the first scene of the fourth act of *La Wally*, where Wally, from the height of the Murzoll, contemplates the sea of ice, 'desolate, infinite, with greenish reflections and solid waves, reaching all the way to the other side of the mountain.' The time and the place made me enjoy redoubled a thousand times the exquisite suggestiveness of that scene, in which the fearful poetry of the glacier is rendered so effectively. Art and reality were fused together, and I was hardly sure whether it was the landscape that had evoked the music's echo or the music that had been materialized into landscape: for a few minutes they were one.

The impression had been so strong and immediate that I promised myself I would write to Catalani about it as soon as I returned to Turin. I knew he was ill, and was happy to think of his pleasure at receiving my letter; for him, sincere praise was like oil for a lamp – the words are his[1] – for he thought of himself as 'made thus: when his spirit was contented, his bodily health was also good.'[2] How could I possibly have imagined that his opera's words would turn out to be so pertinent! 'If it's decreed that I will no longer see the land where I have loved and wept,' Wally exclaims, 'well then, let it be my destiny, I will no longer suffer the pains of this world.'[3] And no longer did Alfredo Catalani suffer them, for since 5 o'clock that morning he had been lying on his deathbed, head emaciated, beautiful, thoughtful eyes closed, thin hands crossed ...

---

1 On 16 August 1884 Catalani wrote to Depanis: 'your letter was like putting oil in a lamp.' Letters 17.

2 Letter of 30 July 1884. Letters 15. Catalani wrote in the first person.

3 Wally's first words in Act Four.

I met Catalani for the first time in 1878. Introduced by Ippolito Valletta[1] and warmly supported by the music editor Giovannina Lucca,[2] who always felt a maternal affection for him, Catalani was soliciting from my late father,[3] then, to his misfortune, impresario of the Teatro Regio, Turin, and Carlo Pedrotti[4] an audition for his opera *Elda*. Such solicitations used to be received every day, and every day witnessed a succession of misunderstood geniuses, each with the inevitable manuscript under his arm. I must confess, and it's the unadorned truth, that I didn't even know Catalani's name, and it was only later that I came to know he had been born on 19 June 1854, in Lucca, into a family that handed down the cult of music from father to son. The father had studied with Pacini[5] and died in 1883; the uncle, Felice Catalani, still lives in Florence, where he teaches music. Alfredo was to become a lawyer or engineer, but on the point of choosing between the law and engines in his sixteenth year,[6] after graduating from high school, the young man, unable

---

1 Ippolito Valletta (or Valetta) was the pen name of the Turin-based Count Giuseppe Ippolito Franchi-Verny (1848–1911), for whom see above, p. 45, n. 3. Depanis's later account of this event makes it clear that Valletta actually came to the theatre with Catalani: see below, p. 111.

2 Giovannina Lucca (1814–94) took over her husband's music publishing business after his death in 1872 and established herself as a formidable presence in the Italian opera world. She published Catalani's *La Falce* in 1875 and effectively mentored his career until her retirement in 1888.

3 Giovanni Depanis (1823–89), who after many years working as an apothecary and devoting his leisure hours to music became impresario of the Teatro Regio in 1876.

4 Pedrotti (1817–93) was a composer and conductor who had been appointed director and conductor of the Teatro Regio in 1868.

5 Giovanni Pacini (1796–1867), a popular and prolific opera composer, most famous for *Saffo* (1840).

6 In fact it was in his eighteenth year: Catalani attended the Liceo Ginnasio Machiavelli in Lucca until August 1871.

to wrong either, abandoned both and threw himself into the arms of music, whom he had secretly flirted with at the classroom desk. Magi,[1] who was to become the director of the Liceo Benedetto Marcello in Venice, taught him the first rudiments, and thanks to the teacher's loving care and the learner's acute perception in just a few months Catalani was able to compose an *Overture*,[2] which was played at the theatre in Lucca, and a *Mass* for four voices and large orchestra performed in the cathedral at Lucca. Early works, yes, but works of a certain value – to the extent that they facilitated Catalani's admission without examination into the Paris Conservatoire of music, where he studied piano with Marmontel and composition with Bazin.[3] In 1873 Catalani returned to Italy, offended because as a foreigner he wasn't allowed to enter the so-called *Prix de Rome*,[4] and following his conscience, which was to become one of his characteristics, rather than knock on every door and take advantage of his Parisian success he continued to study at the Conservatory in Milan under Antonio Bazzini. Making the most of this, he produced *La Falce*, an oriental eclogue with verses by Arrigo Boito, performed in the little theatre of the Conservatory on 25 July 1875[5] as his diploma piece with soprano Italia Giorgio (*Zohra*) and tenor Pietro Resilieri (*Un falciatore*).

---

1 Fortunato Magi (1839–82) who taught at the Istituto Musicale Pacini, Lucca. For more on Magi see *Composer of Lucca*, 33–36 and 92–93.

2 Depanis follows Soffredini in referring to this work as an *Overture*. It appears to be the work that later scholars refer to as a *Sinfonia a Piena Orchestra*.

3 Antoine François Marmontel (1816–98) and François Bazin (1816–78).

4 An annual scholarship allowing a young musician to study in Rome for three to five years, first awarded in 1803. Most of the winners have been completely forgotten, but major figures like Berlioz, Gounod and Bizet had won the *Prix de Rome*.

5 In fact, 19 July.

To many it was a revelation, for others a scandal, for everyone an event. Anathema is what they hurled at the young artist of the future (in those years Milan was inflamed with a sacred horror for Wagner, whose *Lohengrin* had been booed at La Scala[1]), and they came out with the usual contentions about how the singing had been sacrificed to the orchestra and the melody killed by the harmony. I say the usual ones, because they're repeated at every attempt to express musically the meaning of a libretto instead of merely commenting phonically on a simple situation; and because muddling up the *substance* with the *form* of a melody has ever been the vice of partisan criticism. Rereading *La Falce* now, such accusations are bewildering, for how clear the general design appears and how spontaneous the melody; but we must imagine the situation in '75 and recognize that, with his first work of some significance, Catalani showed himself to be animated by a renovating spirit that did not and could not compromise itself to the average Milanese audience's taste, and especially that of the bewigged critics. Reyer, the author of *Sigurd*, *La statue* and *Salambò*, having examined the music, admitted that no young French composer would have been able to achieve the like.[2] This was a valuable admission from a foreign colleague, and not an exaggerated one: it is sufficient to remember the introduction to the eclogue, Zohra's romanza, the flowering of the love duet and the finale in which Zohra and the reaper once again take up *fortissimo* the Mohammedan theme while the caravan goes off into the desert. The polemics lasted for some days, the austere Società del Quartetto granted Catalani the exceptional honour

---

1 The production of *Lohengrin* at La Scala in March 1873 had turned into a fiasco after it encountered intense nationalistic opposition.

2 Ernest Reyer (1823–1909), a French composer and critic, whose operas were very successful in his time. In 1875 he was mainly known for *La statue* (1861). He established himself as a powerful critic in the 1860s. He discussed *La Falce* with Catalani, and expressed the view that 'There isn't a single young man in France who could do as much!' Letters 71.

of performing the symphonic prologue from *La Falce* in its concerts, usually closed to composers at the start of their careers, the young maestro put himself to work again – and soon he was hardly spoken of at all. Outside Milan no one even knew of his existence. The theatrical customs of those days were innocent; the shamelessness of acclaim at any cost and by any means came later.

Catalani's physique was in his favour. He was young – twenty-five[1] – and seemed younger, of average height, slim, slender, his features regular and emphasized by his leanness, with aquiline nose, high, prominent forehead, thick, drooping moustache, and copious, slightly curly black hair. What struck you about him were his eyes sunken under prominent eyebrows: lucid and melancholic, with phosphorescent flashes that penetrated your soul, they were more often staring ecstatically into space as if chasing a remote and languid vision. Catalani used to walk with a slight stoop; he was gentle, timid, abstracted; smiled with a nervous contraction of the lips; laughed rarely, almost convulsively; used to speak with a subdued voice, and would punctuate his words with little bursts of coughing. 'He's catching his soul in his teeth,' the wife of a theatre janitor said of him, and in their common coarseness these words hit the mark.

The musical score Catalani withdrew from his coat partially destroyed the good effect of his person and manners: it was a tall, thick volume, a tower you might say. It was an opera of the fantastic genre in four acts and nine parts, *Elda*. Carlo D'Ormeville had transposed the legend of the Loreley to the banks of the Baltic and constructed upon it a libretto full of fine lines and excellent situations, but prolix and jumbled. Pedrotti asked Catalani how on earth he had dared entangle himself with such a difficult libretto, and Catalani seemed flummoxed by the question, as if surprised by the very idea of difficulty. He sat at

---

[1] In fact Catalani was twenty-four when he met Depanis.

Carlo Pedrotti (1817–93)

the piano and began the prelude: soon we knew we were in the presence of an authentic musician's temperament. He was a first class pianist, giving prominence to the instrumental beauties, but had an impossible voice, shrill, caprine, and incapable of shutting up. Pedrotti was pulling on his beard, growing agitated in his chair, huffing and puffing, begging Catalani to be quiet; to no avail, after a few minutes that harsh voice would return to ruin the effect of the pianistic performance. It was three hours of delight and torment. The benevolence of the listeners had been transformed into admiration; but at the same time the inexperience and exuberance of one starting out, entirely absorbed in his creation and forgetful of the staging and practicalities of performance, were all too evident. 'There's enough music here for two operas,' cried Pedrotti, enthusiastic about the beauty of the score, irritated by its prolixity; and Catalani, more surprised by the praise than the criticism, opened his large eyes wide, clearly taken aback by such qualms as that the artistes would pose difficulties, or that the managers would hesitate before the high cost of scenic arrangements.

For the moment this didn't constitute an obstacle, for my father had a genuine liking for Catalani and was ready to take on the risks of the staging; nevertheless, it was absolutely necessary to lighten certain parts, to retouch others, and to apply the scissors unsparingly everywhere. It was November, and choosing a new opera for the coming carnival season was a matter of urgency, while the modifications had to be made calmly and with proper consideration. So *Die Königin di Saba* by Goldmark was chosen,[1] and *Elda* was postponed until the 1879–80 carnival. Catalani accepted the suggestions gratefully, and did not grow irritated at the delay; rather, he declared himself pleased at the

---

[1] Karl Goldmark (1830–1915) had scored a major success with his first opera, *Die Königin di Saba* (1875), a work which may have influenced *Elda*. The Turin production was the opera's Italian premiere.

choice of *Die Königin di Saba* and returned to Milan with the bulky score that was to be shortened and simplified. 'Modifying is more difficult than creating,' he wrote in December 1878, 'and the time it takes to do it can never be too much.'[1]

Catalani's turn came. The changes were relevant, and the cuts copious, but they weren't enough; the rendering of that Baltic Spirit was as overdone as ever. The artists grumbled, the stagehands grumbled, the suppliers grumbled, – and cuts followed cuts. Tormented in his paternal loins, Catalani would at first protest, then be resigned. The rehearsals for *Elda* were forever famous in the annals of the Regio; the cuts totalled eighteen; little by little a quarter of the score was suppressed. It was a useful lesson for Catalani, and those amputations constituted a practical lesson for which he was always grateful to Pedrotti.

Debuting in a theatre as important as the Regio in Turin, with a director such as Pedrotti, and with a group of celebrated artists such as his[2] was for Catalani a piece of good fortune; but he only had half of it. On the very day of the first performance Barbacini and Bulicioff fell ill. The latter's indisposition was slight and what's more Ulla's role was not of capital importance; but Barbacini's case was very serious and Sveno's role predominant. Between two risks – of putting off the performance after the previous postponements and after rumours had leaked from the rehearsals, or battling on with Barbacini ill and Bulicioff indisposed – it was the second that was snatched at,

---

1 Quoted from Catalani's earliest known letter to Depanis. Letters 1.

2 Depanis has a note here: 'The parts in *Elda* were distributed as follows: *The King of Leira*, Edouard De Reszke; *Ulla*, Nadina Bulicioff; *Sveno*, Enrico Barbacini; *Elda*, Adele Garbini; and *Magno*, Sante Athos.' De Reszke (1853–1917), a Polish bass, was at the beginning of his long and distinguished career, having made his debut as the King in *Aida* in 1876. Bulicioff (1858–1921) was a young Russian soprano, Barbacini (1834–1905) a well-established Italian tenor, Garbini an Italian soprano, Athos an Italian baritone.

and self-denyingly Barbacini decided to sacrifice himself for the maestro.

Oh! that Saturday night of 31 January 1880! On the point of attacking the prelude, the harpist Pinto – may the good man and excellent artist rest in peace – announced to Pedrotti that he felt faint and was not sure he could get to the end of the opera; and don't forget that the harp in *Elda* is utilized heavily, and that the harpist has to move incessantly between orchestra and stage to accompany inset songs and vice versa. I remember I had someone bring a bottle of rich wine to the green room adjacent to the stage, called the 'comforter' in theatrical jargon because it was the place where the maestros used to await their sentence. I was entirely occupied there supporting the weak and sick, supplying a drop to Pinto in the intervals of his peregrinations and a regular drop to Catalani, pale and emotionally exhausted; my father, meanwhile, looked after Barbacini. When the curtain fell on the final scene of the final act, it was a liberation. For the first three acts Barbacini struggled desperately with a stubborn hoarseness that rendered his voice almost tuneless; in the fourth he performed miracles, singing and interpreting the cemetery scene and the love duet in great-artist style.

In the first act, the opera achieved great success, prompting eight calls for the maestro; – it remained good in the first scene of the second, with three calls; it became slightly lukewarm in the third scene of the second act (the second scene suppressed because of Barbacini's illness) and in the entire third act, with four calls; it recovered again during the fourth act, which ended with a triple ovation for Catalani. All in all, a victory, and the more so given that it had been struggled for and gained under such difficult circumstances.

The effort made by Barbacini made his illness worse, and the second performance of *Elda* couldn't take place until the following Saturday, February the seventh; success was confirmed by twenty calls and by an encore for the tenor's romanza. All told the opera was performed a dozen times,[1] was put on again in Warsaw, and everything ended there.

Neither public nor impresarios were wrong; in its original form *Elda* contained seeds of life, but wasn't a living opera, its fault being – as I've already said – overwriting (enviable fault), not anaemia, and that it was too expensive to stage. Catalani himself was fully convinced, and from then on planned further modifications. First, though, he wanted to attempt the stages with a second experiment meant to be a second affirmation of his individuality. The search for a libretto put his patience to the test: 'If you knew how much I think upon a libretto, until I have one in my hands I can't be satisfied,' he said in March 1880,[2] and not having anything better, and overcome by the need to start work again, he accepted one by Zanardini,[3] *Dejanice*, an unhappy reheating of material from

---

[1] Depanis has a note here: 'One of the last performances stood out thanks to an unusual occurrence. The Regio's season ticket holders began to incline towards protesting at the system of presenting new operas, the one thing that gave status to the theatre, but something the complainers designedly supposed or believed to be a sign of meanness. According to these well-informed folk, the new operas didn't really cost anything; rather, the company exploited them!!! May God forgive their foolish falsehood! *Elda*, of course, was taken as a pretext for fresh chatter; but facts followed chatter too, and at the seventh or eighth performance, I don't remember exactly which, from one of the boxes started some timid, low whistles. Just by chance, Catalani was passing along the corridor by the third-row boxes where the plot had been hatched; unrecognized, he overheard. "What have I done to them?" he said to me as a tear formed in his eye; nothing else. In reality, the protesters didn't have anything against either him or *Elda*, but against the company that was "getting fat on the backs of composers"!!! They had wanted to essay their strength, but without result. The attempt was to be more successful the following year with regard to *Carmen*, performances of which they managed to interrupt.' There were in fact nine performances of *Elda*, as Depanis correctly records in his later memoir.

[2] Letter to Depanis of 31 March. Letters 4.

[3] Angelo Zanardini (1820–93), a minor librettist, most important for his translations of foreign librettos, including Verdi's *Don Carlos*.

L'Africana, *Aida* and *La Gioconda* served up in a Greek sauce.¹ The work was performed at La Scala, Milan, on 17 March 1883, with fair success, and was staged again on 21 October 1884 at the Teatro Regio in Turin,² and in the winter of 1886 at the Municipal Theatre in Nice, but it's a dead opera that no revision would be able to galvanize. This is a pity, because although the libretto is indigestible, and often even incomprehensible, and though the structure of the opera is far more conventional than that of *Elda*, from the point of view of the music purely *Dejanice* contains gems of the first water. It is evident that Catalani intended to force his particular temperament so as to respond to the accusations of those who denied his strength; but where he abandons himself to his inspiration, as in the fourth act, he rises to considerable heights, and as a result the musical discourse is tighter and more concise.³

---

1 *Dejanice* is set in ancient Greece.

2 Depanis has a note here: 'The main interpreters of *Dejanice* at La Scala were: Emma Turolla (*Dejanice*) [soprano, 1858–1943]; Lena Bordato *(Argelia)* [soprano]; Edmondo Vergnet (*Admeto*) [French tenor, 1850–1904] who at the performance "gestured" (*accennò*) and didn't sing his part; Giovanni Bianchi (*Dardano*) [baritone] and Francesco Vecchioni (*Labdaco*) [bass]. At the Teatro Regio: Romilda Pantaleoni (*Dejanice*) [soprano, 1847–1917]; Gemma Bellincioni (*Argelia*) [soprano, 1864–1950]; Giovanni Mierzwinsky (*Admeto*) [Wladyslaw Mierzwiński, Polish tenor, 1850–1909] who was not much happier than Vergnet; Delfino Menotti (*Dardano*) [baritone, 1858–1937]; Francesco Vecchioni (*Labdaco*) [bass]. In both theatres the orchestra was directed and conducted by Franco Faccio.' It is remarkable how much stronger the Turin cast was. At the La Scala premiere Vergnet 'gestured' rather than sung because he had lost his voice. See Nappi's account in *Composer of Lucca*, 119–20.

3 The fourth act of *Dejanice* has been consistently the most praised. Jay Nicolaisen judges it 'the best single act Catalani wrote before *La Wally*. ... with just four characters and no chorus to deal with, the composer was able to lay bare the tragic denouement of his story in a single extended monologue, two contrasting duets, and a swift closing scene. There is little recitative, and the composer's lyric inspiration, extended across three set pieces and two notable orchestral passages, leaves one breathless' (156).

From *Dejanice* to *Edmea* Catalani goes through a crisis, and *Edmea* is both the symptom of it and its consequence. High art still holds the same attraction for him, and the symphonic poem *Ero e Leandro*[1] is proof of that; but the composer feels the need for a ready and immediate success that will make him accepted by the crowd and allow him to attempt greater challenges; in other words, he feels the need to have people talk about him. He's been working for eight years: who would dare say he wasn't right? For a moment he paused, pondering whether to set a French libretto for Hartmann;[2] the Franco-Italian relationships being not yet entirely spoiled and many friendships made in Paris among journalists and literates – in particular the Parnassians – made such a project less absurd.[3] But the idea didn't go anywhere. A distinguished artist, Ferni-Germano, kindly pressed him to write an opera for her.[4] Meanwhile, the Scala Management was looking for a short opera to be placed alongside *Amor*, the dance by Manzotti.[5] The opportunity was too good to miss, and Catalani

---

[1] Depanis has a note here: 'Composed in autumn 1884 in Engadine and performed by the Orchestrale Milanese in May 1885.'

[2] Georges Hartmann (1843–1900), an important French music publisher who published the work of many leading French composers. Depanis confuses the chronology here. Catalani had written to him on 24 March 1886, *after* the premiere of *Edmea*, 'Now I want to write an opera on a French libretto. I hope to come to an agreement with Hartmann.' Letters 25.

[3] In February 1888 a decade-long trade war broke out between Italy and France, badly souring relations between the two countries, and having a devastating effect on the Italian economy.

[4] Virginia Ferni-Germano, who created the roles of Edmea and Loreley. *Edmea* was written specially for her (Letters 20). See above, p. 47 n. 1.

[5] Luigi Manzotti (1835–1905), the leading Italian choreographer of this period, was famous for his theatrical extravaganzas. *Amor*, on the history of love through the ages, was described by its creator as a 'great choreographic poem': it featured 200 dancers, even more non-dancing extras, and horses and elephants on the stage. It was premiered at La Scala on 17 February 1886, just ten days before the modestly-scaled *Edmea*.

didn't let it go; he received a libretto from Ghislanzoni,[1] and despite being struck down by illness set himself to working hard, spurred on by the fear of dying before he had accomplished it; *Edmea* was ready for the carnival of 1886. The first performance took place on 27 February at La Scala, Milan; the critics expressed some not entirely incorrect reservations, the public adopted an air of obduracy, but increasingly over sixteen evenings came success. *Edmea*, put on again in the summer in Trento and in the autumn at the Carignano theatre in Turin,[2] made the rounds of the principal theatres in the peninsula and travelled abroad, even as far as Russia. It achieved its goal for the composer, and made Catalani better known than his previous operas had; but it doesn't constitute his true claim to fame.

In *Edmea* Catalani is rapid and concise, the former uncertainties and prolixity have disappeared, the composer's aim is right on target and he doesn't dawdle on his way. He has not succumbed to the seduction of grand spectacles based on marches, grand finales and electrical light; first among the young opera composers, he intuits that it is possible to benefit enormously from choosing an intimate drama of modest proportions, and thus accepts his descent from the clouds of legend, finding accents

---

1 Antonio Ghislanzoni (1824–93), mainly remembered for his libretto for *Aida*.

2 Depanis has a note here: 'The main interpreters of *Edmea* in Milan were Virginia Ferni-Germano (*Edmea*), Gaetano Ortisi (*Oberto*) [tenor, 1844–1929], Francesco Pozzi (*Ulmo*) [baritone]; at Turin, first performance, which was a triumph, on 4 November 1886, Ferni-Germano (*Edmea*), Nikolai Figner (*Oberto*) [distinguished Russian tenor, 1857–1918], Senatore Sparapani (*Ulmo*) [baritone, 1847–1926]; second performance, 4 May 1889, Ernestina Bendazzi-Garulli (*Edmea*) [soprano, 1864–1931], Oreste Emiliani (*Oberto*) [tenor, b. 1856], and Edoardo Sottolana (*Ulmo*) [baritone]. In Milan the director was Franco Faccio; at Turin, in both performances, Arturo Toscanini, debuting with *Edmea* at the Carignano theatre, rehearsed the singers and orchestra.' For Virginia Ferni-Germano, one of the most important early interpreters of Catalani's music, see above, p. 47 n. 1.

so delicate that Ferrettini rightly defined them as like Bellini's.[1] Who doesn't remember, for example, the tender, sweet, little duet from the third act, 'You are here? On my breast?', which had audiences on their feet everywhere?[2] But the conventionality of the proceedings, not vulgarity which is unknown to Catalani, and the lesser originality of melodic invention, which in the second finale has connections with *La Gioconda* and *Mefistofele* and in the third finale with *Faust*, show the intrinsic weakness of the score. *Edmea* is a transitional opera which many a composer would be glad to acknowledge his own, and for Catalani it marks a phase independent of both his earliest tendencies and subsequent evolution. This he felt, and the continuing success surprised and almost ended up annoying him, as *Elda* and *Dejanice* were forgotten and he was addressed as the author of *Edmea* alone.

Meanwhile, unstable health forbidding his applying himself to sustained work, and the usual lack of a good libretto, made Catalani return to the old idea of redoing *Elda*, stripping it of the beggar's clothes that had permitted the Loreley of the Rhine to be transformed into a Baltic Fairy, and giving back to the legend its real meaning. D'Ormeville, Zanardini and Illica[3] helped him in this exhausting but not unpleasant task: it was still his first offspring beaming at him from those papers, blonde, fascinating, seductive, and with plenty of freshness and youth flowing from her song! In February 1887 Catalani wrote from Venice: 'My wish is to return to Milan to continue my work on *Loreley*; it will be twenty times superior to *Edmea*, which I'm getting

---

[1] Ernesto Ferrettini, music critic for the *Gazzetta Piemontese*. He was not the first to compare Catalani's music to Bellini's (Nicolaisen 154).

[2] Depanis actually misquotes: the libretto has 'Tu sei quì – sul mio cor' ('You are here – on my heart'); Depanis writes 'sen' for 'cor.' It is an affirmative statement rather than a question. *Edmea* (Milan, 1886), 42.

[3] For Illica, see above, p. 49 n. 7.

tired of.'[1] In the April of the same year he went to Florence 'in order to finish *Loreley*, which will be my best work';[2] and on 17 November 1887 *Loreley* was finished. 'I am persuaded that *Loreley*, redone in this way, will become a fairy deserving of respect, so long as she's willing to travel the world in search of money for her papa.'[3] Honest wish, which was to remain long unfulfilled. For two years, while many mediocrities infested the Italian scene, a maestro who could be proud of successes such as *La Falce*, *Elda*, *Dejanice* and *Edmea* couldn't find a theatre willing to open its doors to his *Loreley*.[4]

Those two years were characterized by inaction and discouragement, wasted in looking for a libretto and an impresario. In the meantime, the explosions named *Le Villi* and *Asrael* had appeared,[5]

---

1 Letter of 22 February 1887. Letters 38.

2 Letter of 30 April 1887. Letters 40.

3 Letter of 2 January 1887: Letters 35.

4 Depanis misrepresents the case: the main reason for the long delay was that in spring 1888, Catalani's publisher, Giovannina Lucca, sold her business to her rival, Giulio Ricordi, who thus acquired the rights to Catalani's operas. Ricordi was much more intent on promoting Puccini's career than Catalani's, so *Loreley* had to wait on the former's long-delayed *Edgar* (which premiered disastrously in April 1889). In the meantime, it was impossible for any theatre to choose to bring out Catalani's opera. For more on this, see *Composer of Lucca*, 21–23.

5 Depanis's chronology is shaky. *Le Villi*, Puccini's first opera, was written for the 1883 Sonzogno competition, in which it failed to obtain even an honourable mention (because of Puccini's virtually illegible score, it has been suggested). Nevertheless, friends and well-wishers organized a performance that took place on 31 May 1884; *Le Villi* then proved a great success, and critics enjoyed pouring scorn on the Sonzogno jury. Ricordi purchased the opera, which was quite widely performed in the mid-1880s, just before *Edmea* conquered Italy. Alberto Franchetti's first opera, *Asrael*, was premiered on 11 February 1888. It was a huge success, and for a time established Franchetti as Catalani's most formidable rival among the younger Italian composers.

and the crowd's curiosity was attracted by the novelty of two new names, which the injustice of a competition in Puccini's case and his father's millions in Franchetti's made all the more appealing. Vindicating a disparaged genius and giving homage to a youngster for whom riches are a stimulus, not an impediment, to work: these are acts honouring the comprehension of the public. Catalani didn't react to these just honours, suffering only the negative impact they had on *Loreley*, condemned to enforced inaction. 'Lucky him, marrying knowledge and money!' he would say of Franchetti,[1] and if the astonishing orchestra gathered for *Asrael* in Florence suggested to him the innocent joke that 'there were enough strings to hang half the world's population,'[2] of *Cristoforo Colombo* he wrote: 'You'll be flabbergasted by the instrumentation. It seems impossible that in fifty-six days one could set five acts to music with such a confident, balanced touch, and with colours that are always beautiful, full, and dazzling.'[3] Puccini's successes and later Mascagni's and Leoncavallo's made him exclaim: 'Lucky them, able to knock in the nail; I haven't been able to do it at all!'[4] Sad exclamation, which doesn't offend anyone, and which is the acknowledgement of a very much sadder truth, the resigned protest of a genius aware of his own value and who finds himself isolated and, worse, thwarted. Hadn't the modest

---

1 Letter of 17 February 1888. Letters 47.

2 Letter of 18 April 1889. Letters 62.

3 *Cristoforo Colombo*, Franchetti's second opera, premiered on 6 October 1892. Catalani admired it a great deal: see *Composer of Lucca*, 123. The quotation here is from a letter to Depanis of 30 September 1892. Letters 118. The published letter says 36 days, and was possibly mistranscribed by Carlo Gatti, who published Catalani's letters to Depanis in 1946.

4 The statement comes from a letter of 28 February 1893, where it refers only to Puccini; Depanis adapts it to give it a wider meaning: see *Composer of Lucca*, 61 n. 1.

success of *Edmea*'s premiere excited the animus of some compassionate colleagues to the point of toasting Catalani's 'fiasco,' greeting it as a welcome event? It was the impudence of cocky and excitable young men, I don't deny, but it was enough to affect the spirit of an artist searching around for sympathy, that precious stimulus to creation, and finding indifference or hostility instead.

In those awful years the situation regarding the competition for the chair in composition at the Conservatory in Milan, vacant since Amilcare Ponchielli's death, contributed to the embitterment of Catalani's existence.[1] Independent by nature, he wasn't at all suited to teaching; but the career of a composer didn't appear at all profitable, he wasn't rich, and had to think of providing his own bread. Three thousand lira a year was enough to survive.[2] He hesitated a long time, let pass two competitions that produced no result, and stood in the third one. On merit, he was the first in the group of three names submitted by the selection panel to the Minister of Public Instruction, but the state of his health was made an issue, touching a note that sounded most painful to him. Among the criticisms made of *Edmea*, one in particular had struck him to the heart: the one characterizing his as anaemic music by an anaemic maestro. Now the Ministry's hesitation, prompted by fears that his uncertain health might leave him unable to fulfil the obligations of a professor, added salt to the old wound. And on 28 March 1888 he wrote (I often quote his very words because his letters mirror all that passed through his head, whether pleasant or unpleasant, whether good or bad,

---

1 Ponchielli died on 16 January 1886, and Catalani was finally appointed his successor on 11 April 1888. However, as Catalani did not compete in the first two competitions, it would appear that he could not have entered his application before 1887.

2 This was the salary attached to the professorship.

and I'm trying to delineate the profile of a soul rather than the biography of an artist): on 28 March he wrote: 'I'd be the first to resign if I saw that my health were an obstacle ... I wouldn't be at all surprised if, bit by bit, my opponents managed to convince the Ministry that I'm a poor consumptive *in extremis*. It would be much harder on me not to have the post for this reason, than for being a proven ass. At least I could still prove that I'm not an ass!'[1] Any comment would weaken the effect of this final phrase, containing a sea of troubles. And how we understand that desperate cry: 'I'm tired of this artistic life of mine that neither morally nor materially gives me what it ought to! So be it!'[2] And we understand the bile tormenting him: 'I don't deny I have bile in my soul, given what happens, and I'm terrified at the thought of what might be my future ... Oh! What a comedy the world is and what a bad one! And how tired I am of it!'[3]

Catalani won in the end, thanks to generous support. Appointed as professor on a trial basis for a year, he was definitively confirmed before the end of it. But this victory was not a happy one, the combat had shattered him, and a train of bitterness concerning it remained in his mind: amid threats from illness his vision of life became darker and more desolate.

The production of *Loreley* at the Regio in Turin[4] was, once again, only half fortunate; it brought the score out from the oblivion in which it had languished, and it infused in the maestro some hope and activity, but its promise couldn't be maintained. Comparison between the old *Elda* and new *Loreley*, on the very

---

1 Letters 50. Depanis combines extracts from letters of 28 and 31 March.
2 Letter of 20 January 1887. Letters 36.
3 Letter of 20 August 1889. Letters 65.
4 *Loreley* was premiered there on 16 February 1890.

stage that nine years earlier had welcomed the earlier work, promised to be curious and artistically interesting; moreover, *Edmea* had achieved popular support for Catalani. Everything seemed as if it ought to come together in a great success. But no. The Regio had been contracted to a Society of gentlemen, full of excellent intentions but too large to be able to produce among its members the harmony and unity of concept essential in a theatre production: each stakeholder, in his position as a co-owner, had his own project and his own predilections that he wished to see triumph. The result was petty wars, dissensions, and compromises that achieved nothing and even aggravated the situation. There were jealousies and spites – both of which, to make things worse, leaked out to the public, the less favourable rumours always concerning the pretended indiscretions of the 'Impresarios': about a hundred of them. As if that weren't enough, there then followed a sequel of calamities unequalled in living memory: the death of my poor father, head of the Society, on the very eve of the theatre's opening,[1] the *influenza* raging among artists and crowds, so that in a month only seven performances were staged, all incomplete, followed by the death of Prince Amadeo[2] and the subsequent temporary closure of the theatre, – all this had created a cold, moody, almost hostile atmosphere, a thousand miles from the serenity needed to judge a work of art properly.

The *Loreley* rehearsals had dragged on discouragingly slowly, the result of circumstances rather than will, and the drawn-out changes redoubled the rumours that there must be something rotten if so much time and effort were needed to stage an opera that wasn't even new: and that *Loreley* oughtn't

---

1 Giovanni Depanis died on 11 November 1889.

2 Amadeo I (1845–90), Duke of Aosta and briefly King of Spain. Resident in Turin for most of his life, he died there on 18 January 1890, a month before the premiere of *Loreley*.

to be considered a new opera was the main accusation levelled against Catalani's latest work. Misfortunes never come singly, as Catalani knew well, the victim of faults not his own. On the afternoon of the day fixed for the dress rehearsal, Durot, the tenor, fell ill, and to avoid further delays it had to be done without him, and as a consequence behind closed doors so as to avoid giving the disastrous impression that those present would receive. To no avail. The measure painfully imposed by the circumstances was implemented with scrupulous inflexibility, and this provoked protests on the part of those who usually attended rehearsals: protests from the impresario stakeholders who saw themselves stripped of what they believed – and, within certain limits, were – their rights; and protests from the artists who saw the doors inexorably closed to family members. When it comes to rehearsals, the families of artists acquire a frightening elasticity.

As God willed it, the first performance took place on the evening of 17 February 1890, the Sunday before Carnival, in front of an audience that was either diffident or distracted.[1] The tacit hostility, slithering about the stalls and more pronounced in the boxes, had no way of expressing itself. The first act was received with unanimous applause; the second, thanks in part to the uncertainty of the artist, a beginner, given the role of *Anna*, passed in silence; the third reestablished a success that four final calls for Catalani put the seal on. The maestro abstained from appearing on stage with the curtain up; his example, rather than being praised and imitated, offered a weapon to his adversaries, who broadcast to the four winds that the curtains calls had been less than ten and, it was implied, that the opera had been booed: successes, according to this latest system, are calculated on the basis of the *encores*

---

1 Depanis has the date wrong, but the day right. The premiere was actually on 16 February, which was a Sunday.

and kilometres of calls.¹ The following performances proved the pessimistic forecasts and compassionate telegrams wrong; from the second performance even Act Two was enjoyed and *Loreley* closed the season very much more brilliantly than it had begun.

With *Loreley* Catalani took a decisive step, abandoning the conventionalism that in *Edmea* was sheltering ill-concealed behind the refinements of the music; in *Loreley* the musical discourse only suffers rare interruptions and the drama reigns supreme. The composer's personality is asserted in the disdain of vulgar little effects, in the nobility of the general design, in the conciseness of the development which from the beginning of Act Two seems almost excessively condensed, in the elegant limpidity of the idea. And there was a Roman critic who dared print that *Loreley* didn't say anything new, when that critic hadn't even attended a performance of the opera!² The critic is dead, and forgiveness is required for such a superficiality

---

1 Depanis has a note here: 'The main roles in *Loreley* were played by the following: *Rodolfo*, Natale Pozzi [bass]; *Anna*, Eleonora Dexter [soprano, described by Depanis as 'a beginner']; *Walter*, Eugenio Durot [tenor, d. 1908]; *Loreley*, Virginia Ferni-Germano [soprano]; *Hermann*, Enrico Stinco-Palermini [baritone]. Conductor and orchestra director, Edoardo Mascheroni.' For Durot and Ferni-Germano, both of whom attended Catalani's funeral, see above, p. 49 n. 11 and p. 47 n. 1 respectively. The expression 'kilometres of calls' is perhaps worth remark: if read literally it presumably refers to the distance traversed by the maestro in his walks on and off stage. Depanis's note continued with a long account of how *Elda* had been adapted as *Loreley*. This appears below as an appendix, pp. 108–9.

2 The critic in question was Francesco d'Arcais (1830–90). Catalani was incensed by his review of *Loreley*, writing to Depanis on 4 April 1890: 'I ask you to let me know if you know if the illustrious d'Arcais went to Turin to hear *Loreley*. If he did, he has every right to express whatever judgment, but if not (as I, positively, believe), I won't forgive him for the article in the *Nuova Antologia*, which would be real wickedness, to say nothing else. It must take a fine spirit to speak poorly of a work without having heard it, and to say that there's nothing "new!"' Letters 80.

as this, which offended Catalani in his *amour-propre* and his interests; but we can't understand how the simple reading of Act Three of *Loreley* failed to halt the critic's pen, unless he hadn't read the music just as he hadn't heard it. Among the many young composers' scores which have seen the light in Italy during the last twenty years I don't know one that can boast an act to place beside the third in *Loreley*, undoubtedly the maestro's most inspired.[1]

When *Loreley* was selected for Turin, Catalani had already set his eyes on a new libretto; inactivity weighed upon him and at whatever cost he was determined to avoid it, even without the help of a publisher. He aspired to treat a simple and simultaneously grand subject: 'I have in view a splendid subject,' he wrote from Cernobbio on 6 September 1886, 'with large scenes, without the conventional duets, trios or quartets. It's by Illica. I assure you that it's new, original and elevated.'[2] But it was a false hope, nor can we suppose that the reference is to *La Wally* because in the following winter Catalani writes again: 'I'm pondering and studying to find a subject that is really beautiful for a new opera. Wasted effort! I can't find anything. I've got to the point where I'd be willing to write an opera for free, provided I was given a

---

[1] Depanis has a note here: 'After a pause of exactly two years, *Loreley* was performed again in Genoa on 17 February 1892 with complete success that only increased in Rome on 7 February 1893 and turned into hysteria in Palermo on 12 February of the same year.' It is interesting to note that Toscanini, Catalani's friend and champion, shared Depanis's view that the third act of *Loreley* was Catalani's greatest: see Tobia Nicotra, *Arturo Toscanini*, trans. Irma Brandeis and H. D. Kahn (New York, 1929), 84.

[2] Letters 29. I am not aware that the significance of this letter has ever been remarked. Illica was working as a playwright in the 1880s. His first libretto to be set was *Il Vassallo di Szigeth* (1889) for Antonio Smareglia, and it was only in the early 1890s that he really established himself as a librettist. The libretto Catalani writes of here was thus a very early effort, and it seems likely that it was abandoned by Illica.

good libretto. Who will give me one? Who will give me one?'[1] Right at the beginning of 1888 I find a hint regarding the novel *Wally the Vulture* (*Die Geier-Wally*) by Wilhelmine von Hillern, published in the appendices to *La Perseveranza*, overflowing with strong and dramatic situations.[2] Illica draws a libretto from it that pleases Arrigo Boito and Giuseppe Giacosa, and seduces Catalani, who plans to set it to music in two years. In January 1891 he shares the good news that the music is practically done, a question of two or three months further effort thanks to the hard work and inspiration that weren't lacking, and he adds: 'I hope I haven't created ugly music … It seems to me it's coming out well. It's a true musical drama (at times a comedy), without detachable pieces, without grand finales for effect and without choruses for padding.'[3] In May *La Wally* is finished. After an audition, Giulio Ricordi, the owner of the editorial firm Francesco Lucca,[4] purchases the opera, which he judges 'fast-moving, interesting, vigorous and full of youth.'[5] And it's not too long before *La Wally* appears on the list of the Scala Theatre Company

---

[1] Letter of 20 January 1887. Letters 36.

[2] This seems to be a simple error; if not, it is a mysterious statement. There is no 'hint' concerning *Wally* in Catalani's published letters of early 1888, and it seems clear that he was not contemplating an opera derived from the novel at that time. He (apparently) first mentioned the subject to Depanis on 1 September 1888: 'If you have the *Perseveranza* from last year, I ask you to read a story, translated from the German, entitled *Wally the Vulture*, which appeared in that paper, it seems to me, in the months of July and August. It seems to me that there are strong situations in that story that could lend themselves to an opera libretto.' Letters 53. The idea had come from Boito in the summer: see *Composer of Lucca*, 126–30.

[3] Depanis combines statements from letters of 1 January 1891 and a few weeks later. Letters 83, 84.

[4] As noted above, Ricordi had bought the Lucca company in spring 1888.

[5] Catalani reported Ricordi's opinion to Depanis in a letter of 24 June 1891. Letters 88.

in Milan for the carnival of 1891–92. Perhaps fortune is about to smile on Catalani?

Perhaps, but no. The rehearsals tire a rather ill Catalani, some rumours of editorial vendettas – demonstrated to be groundless – and certain stings from colleagues disturb him and make him nervous; he feels more isolated than ever and the target of immense envy despite how barely enviable his condition is; and he paints everything black, and has doubts about himself and about his opera: 'The opera flows, I don't think it's boring,' he writes on 16 January, 'but it might not be liked.'[1] The gloomy forecasts don't come true. *La Wally* triumphs from the start with the public,[2] and with *Tannhäuser* shares the honour of saving the season. But if the public acclaims the maestro, the critics are not disarmed: they acknowledge *La Wally*'s success with gritted teeth and display a singular severity.

The Wagnerian fetishism was at its fiercest. Wagner was the idol, there was nothing else beyond Wagner. The operas of Wagner were the infallible touchstone. And the critics would lecture at Catalani, imparting their suggestions in the form of floggings; they complained of not finding in *La Wally* the wide flow of the Wagnerian wave, and in the name of Wagner they hurled thunderbolts at the quartet in the second act as

---

1 Letter of 16 January 1892. Letters 97.

2 Depanis has a note here: 'The main interpreters of *La Wally* at La Scala on 20 January 1892 were: *Wally*, Hariclea Darclée [Romanian soprano, 1860–1939]; *Stromminger*, Ettore Brancaleoni [bass]; *Afra*, Virginia Guerrini [mezzo-soprano, 1871–1948]; *Walter*, Adelina Stehle [Austrian soprano, 1860–1945]; *Giuseppe Hagenbach*, Emanuele Suagnes [tenor]; *Vincenzo Gellner*, Arturo Pessina [baritone, 1858–1926]; *Old Soldier*, Pietro Cesari [bass, 1847–1922, specializing in comic roles]. Conductor, Edoardo Mascheroni. After Milan, *La Wally* was performed at the Giglio Theatre, Lucca, on 4 September 1892, at the Carlo Felice Theatre, Genoa, on 16 October 1892, and at the Comunale Theatre, Hamburg, on 16 February 1893.' For Hariclea Darclée, see above, p. 46 n. 6.

if Wagner hadn't composed the quintet in *Die Meistersinger* and the trio in *Götterdämmerung!* The curious thing is that at bottom the Milanese critics were not hostile to Catalani, and they would have liked to raise an altar to counter Mascagni; but they couldn't forgive Catalani for not slavishly following the cart of Bayreuth triumphant, and would meticulously fault-search his material without realizing that this was in the interest of his opponents. At the first performance few among the journalists had the courage to judge *La Wally* a vital opera, G. B. Nappi of *La Perseveranza* being among the few;[1] but after seeing the public's approval entirely undiminished over sixteen performances, and examining the score more carefully, most changed their minds, and now it's widely accepted that *La Wally* is the best balanced and most homogeneous work of the maestro.

Catalani suffered incredibly from the behaviour of part of the press and the manners of some of his colleagues toward him; he'd accept criticism gratefully and would benefit from it, changing, as he did, various pieces from *Loreley* and *La Wally*; but he was offended by those who tried to insist that he should abandon his own convictions. 'After all,' he'd sigh, 'having a style of one's own must surely be of some value!' And he was tormented at finding himself demoted to the second rank, and the Mascagnian racket (*gazzarra*) inflamed him: not against Mascagni, but against the takeover of public and theatres managed in favour of the maestro from Leghorn.[2] Then he'd repeat his earlier complaints against a destiny that would not cease

---

[1] Giovanni Battista Nappi (1857–1932), whose important 1918 essay on Catalani is included in *Composer of Lucca*.

[2] Mascagni's *Cavalleria Rusticana* had its epoch-making premiere at the Teatro Costanzi, Rome, on 17 May 1890, and was soon being played all over Italy. The timing was particularly bad for Catalani, who had finally seen *Loreley* staged just three months earlier.

stinging him – he'd have preferred an open battle –, and he used to have rebellious rages that made others smile at him who was so mild: 'I'm living like a patient snail, that for the moment keeps its horns inside, ready to put them out at the first occasion, and then, I hope, they will have become so hard and long as to transfix at least a couple of critics.'[1] A disgust at art would assail him, and between serious and facetious he would cry: 'Believe me, if only I could change my job. Do you want to employ me at your brickyard? I can assure you I will perform my duty well, and won't get distracted! I will be a model employee. At least I'll have enough bricks handy to smash the brains of those who don't have any!'[2] And he would declare that he didn't want to write another line of music; it's cruel when you work with honest artistic intentions and then realize it was, and is, pointless: 'even writing a masterpiece you run the risk of either not being heard, or being pitied.'[3]

These were only short-lived moments of discouragement; soon Catalani would be back to himself and a desire for battle would rise again and push him into action: 'For God's sake, I've been working for twelve years, and should I calmly sit and watch my place taken from me? Definitely not!'[4]

So working was very important, and, in order to work, a libretto – the eternal obstacle encountered in his path. Catalani had deluded himself that Arrigo Boito would help him in these difficulties: 'If this came true, it would be a great benefit for me, as only with a libretto by Boito would I be able to do the precise work I feel I can do and I want to do. It is really about time I had a *total* stroke of luck, rather than

---

[1] Letter of 3 August 1890 (the letter Depanis reproduces in facsimile in his 1915 account of Catalani). Letters 81.
[2] Ibid.
[3] Letter of 19 November 1892. Letters 122.
[4] Letter of 26 January 1893. Letters 128.

half a one, as has always happened to me up to now.'[1] But Boito was distracted by other commitments, and Catalani, fretting in his enforced rest, wrote to me: 'You who read a lot' (unfortunately!) 'could you put me in the way to find a subject I could set to music? It's a serious matter. I don't know where to look. Is there nothing to take from the Russian novels?'[2] And he would reaffirm: 'I'm not happy because I'm not working. My health is much better than usual' (it was 16 May 1892), 'and that makes me regret even more that I don't have a libretto ready to work on. I can't find one. It's a serious matter, it's desperate. And if you think among composers there's one that reads, it's me!'[3]

The idea of creating an opera from Loti's novel *Pêcheur d'Islande* (Iceland Fisherman) occurred to him; but he gave it up because of the overwhelming uniformity of the action.[4] He similarly renounced Theuriet's *La Chanoinesse* because the rumour that Alberto Franchetti was meditating an *André Chénier* had spread,[5] and the two operas would both have been set during the French Revolution. Illica tried to help him with a *Russalka* taken from a story by Sacher-Masoch, that was eventually discarded after

---

[1] Depanis combines statements from Catalani's letters of 18 May 1888 and 1 September 1888. Letters 52, 53.

[2] Letter of 10 March 1892. Letters 103.

[3] Depanis combines statements from letters of 16 May 1892 and 11 April 1893. Letters 106, 131.

[4] According to Carlo Paladini, another friend of Catalani's, Catalani was actually very serious about making an opera from Pierre Loti's *Pêcheur d'Islande* (1886) and entered into an extensive correspondence with the author (*Composer of Lucca*, 144–46). Catalani's stated reason for abandoning the project was simply 'I need other colours.' Letters 123.

[5] *La Chanoinesse*, a novel of the French Revolution by André Theuriet (1833–1907), had been published in early 1893. Catalani reported its operatic potential to Depanis on 11 April (Letters 131) – a good example of how up-to-date he was with developments in the literary world.

much hesitation,[1] and with another libretto inspired by a novel of Tolstoy's. Last June, completely happy, Catalani wrote: 'My new opera will be in three acts and the title will be: *Nella Selva* (*In the woods*). The culminating scene is from Tolstoy. Hillern too is producing a libretto for me.[2] What is certain is I really feel like working, and so I search, and cannot find a suitable location.'[3] Alas! A month later I received a postcard, the final one, in which he told me: 'I didn't get in contact with you because I haven't been well for the last fifteen days. First I had an *abscess* in my mouth, cruelly tormenting me. Now I find myself in a state of great weakness, having lost my appetite. I'm sure the great heat also contributes.'[4] It wasn't the great heat, no, nor the abscess in his mouth; on 2 August a violent gush of blood caught him while he was travelling toward the San Gottard pass and forced his return to Milan;[5] on the seventh the sacrifice was complete, and in my absence the following telegram was delivered, terrible in its laconic tone: 'Most distraught communicate loss maestro

---

1 The only mention of this project in the letters to Depanis comes on 26 November 1892: 'Illica says he'll make me an outline based on the story by Sacher and Masoch, which I like.' Letters 123. Leopold Sacher-Masoch (1836–95), about whom Catalani was clearly confused, was an Austrian writer, famous for his stories of sexual perversion. He wrote many stories with Ukrainian or Russian settings, and it seems likely that Catalani had come across one of these. The legend of the *russalki*, or *rusalki*, had already been given operatic treatment in Russia, most notably by Alexander Dargomïzhsky.

2 Wilhelmine von Hillern, author of the novel on which *La Wally* had been based.

3 Letter of 20 June 1893. Letters 136.

4 Letter of 6 July 1893. Letters 137. There was in fact a later postcard: Depanis mentions this below, p. 107.

5 According to Catalani's later biographer, Severino Pagani, Catalani was travelling to Faido in Switzerland: *Alfredo Catalani: Ombre e luci nella sua Vita e nella sua Arte* (Milan, 1957), 168.

Catalani. Funeral: Wednesday nine o'clock.' Poor Alfredo was looking for a suitable place to work: death had found it for him.

By way of artistic legacy, passing over in silence the youthful works mentioned above, Alfredo Catalani leaves many pieces for pianoforte; several romanzas; a quartet for strings; a symphonic poem, *Ero and Leandro*; a *Scherzo* and a *Contemplazione* performed by the Milan Orchestra at the Trocadero, Paris, in 1878; the oriental eclogue *La Falce*, in one act, libretto by Tobia Gorrio (Arrigo Boito); *Elda*, a lyric drama in four acts, libretto by Carlo D'Ormeville, which became *Loreley* in three acts; *Dejanice* in four acts, libretto by Angelo Zanardini; *Edmea* in three acts, libretto by Antonio Ghislanzoni; *La Wally* in four acts, libretto by Luigi Illica. It's quite a lot for a maestro who did not reach forty, though not as much as Catalani could have done in normal circumstances, for he was hard-working and had a spontaneous vein. His weak health, the ever-recurring lack of a libretto, and the cares of teaching at the Conservatory were what prevented there being more.

Catalani hadn't underestimated his task as a professor. He was protective of his students, 'woe betide him who touches them!' he used to say, and he didn't flee from making sacrifices on their behalf; to make space for a piece by one of them, during a symphonic concert, he declared that he would withdraw his own composition, substituting it with the student's.[1] His maxim was to allow each student to follow his own temperament, and to those who regarded this as a dangerous policy, he'd reply: 'If a student of mine feels like that, why should I derail him? All genres in music are good, as long as *heartfelt* and *well played*.'[2] And

---

[1] The student in question was Federico Salerni, and the composition seems to have been a symphonic poem, *La Tempesta*. Letters 65, 68.

[2] Letter of 3 August 1890 (the letter Depanis later printed in facsimile). Letters 81. Catalani was actually referring specifically to criticism for letting students 'indulge a little too much in the so-called areas of the future.'

with his method he obtained excellent results; Salerni, Tarenghi, Mariani, Gatti and Luporini[1] attest positively to the maestro and will maintain, let's hope, the prestige of the school from which they came.[2]

But even at the cost of calling upon myself a landslide of objections and protests I don't want to, and shouldn't, restrain myself from asserting that Catalani with his own works, independent of his teaching, was the founder of what should be called the Tuscan school. When *Le Villi* by Puccini was

---

1 Federico Salerni (b. 1864), composer; Mario Tarenghi (1870–1938), composer and teacher; Eligio Mariani (dates unknown), composer; Carlo Gatti (1876–1965), later Professor at the Milan Conservatory and author of biographies of Verdi and Catalani; Gaetano Luporini (1865–1948), composer and teacher, later director of the Istituto Musicale Pacini in Lucca. Of this group it was Luporini, who had graduated in 1891, who had made much the biggest impact: indeed Catalani had come to regard him as something of a rival (Letters 133).

2 Depanis has a note here: 'Since we're talking of Catalani the teacher here, it won't be unpleasant to those who cherish the memory of Carlo and Sigismondo Rossaro if I reproduce part of a letter concerning them. Carlo Rossaro, who died in 1878, had left an unfinished opera, *Cassandra*, based on a poem by his son Sigismondo. The latter, who had graduated as an engineer and not attended regular studies in any Lyceum or Conservatory, put himself forward to complete his father's opera; helped by a decided aptitude for music, but troubled by poor health, he studied harmony, composition and arranging by himself, and did what he'd promised himself, finishing and arranging his father's opera; then, exhausted by the effort, he died. Catalani had the chance to examine the score, and this is what he wrote: "That poor son of Rossaro seems to me marvellous in his orchestrating, and for the will power and talent he demonstrates, given the particular conditions of both his health and experience. There are defects, and many. But what matter? I think *Cassandra* would deserve to be performed (apart from the music's deserts) if for no other reason than to pay homage to the memory of a man who, in my opinion, is one of the best examples of the saying: if you want to you can."' Depanis quotes a letter of 22 November 1888. Letters 54. Carlo Rossaro is described at length in Depanis's essay, 'How I Became a Wagnerian.'

performed in Hamburg the critics recognized the points of contact it had with the later *Cavalleria Rusticana* by Mascagni; *Le Villi*, in turn, is linked with *Elda*, which as well as technical, musical analogies shows analogies of situation, subject and colour; and some episodes in *Manon Lescaut* derive from *La Wally*, for example the song of the lamplighter which is sister in flesh and blood to the Bacchic song sung by the Old Soldier. By this, I don't mean to suggest that Puccini copied from Catalani and Mascagni from Puccini and Catalani; parenthood doesn't mean plagiarism. I only intend to underline the relationship, or affinity if preferred, that connects Catalani with Puccini from Lucca and Mascagni from Leghorn: a Tuscan trio in which, if the prognoses are confirmed, the pupil – Luporini, also from Lucca – will come to replace the maestro. And if Catalani with *La Falce* and *Elda* was the first to establish himself, it's fair to place him as head of the school that later came into being.

Far be it from me to deliver a judgment upon Catalani's entire oeuvre; I'll just try to define some of its aspects. Among the most prominent is elegance of form, together with fluidity of invention; the outlines of his music are dressed in the sharply-defined purity of Tuscan landscapes. Catalani's Muse is aristocratic, not mannered; his melody clear, not vulgar; his understanding solid and assimilated, not on display. He abhorred showing off and pursued an ideal of simplicity, which is where he located the true secret of art. He has been criticized for a tendency to use minor tones, giving his music a melancholy stamp; but if such a tendency cannot be denied, it's equally true that it has been exaggerated by his critics, and that the maestro's health induced him to recognize and exaggerate it himself. On the other hand, it's an absurd pretence to expect an artist to give up his own way of feeling, that's to say his own personality, to mould himself upon the latest model of criticism, or worse, the latest caprice of a critic. To one side of a Rossini and a Verdi there's space for a Bellini, and the law of contrasts is the law of life.

Catalani, of a contemplative nature, understood the fantastic as few in Italy; but he didn't understand just the fantastic, and *La Wally* is a human drama in which the realism of the representation develops in an ambience that's not without its touch of mystery.[1] There are two chords that Catalani was able to touch with a particular mastery: love and nature. All his operas have women's names.[2] He was the singer of woman *par excellence*, and in expressing her aspirations his notes had the softness of kisses, and an exquisite sweetness; his love isn't passion, it's sentiment, and aims high and far: a shiver runs through it; almost an arcane voice from the beyond. Perhaps no one in Italy identified himself with nature like Catalani and felt and rendered landscape so effectively, helped as he was in this by his mastery of orchestration and knowledge of nuances: the four acts of *La Wally* are admirable for their suitable and appropriate colouring, and no canvas will be able to express the poem of the glacier like the prelude to the fourth act. From the same pictorial ability derives the excellence of the episodic choruses distributed through his operas with unusually refined criteria for their occasioning: the chit-chat in *Edmea*, the chorus of the old maidens in *Loreley*, of the courtesans in *Dejanice*, of the hunters in *La Wally*, and so on. But, let me repeat, I've no intention of entering into a minute examination of Catalani's music; although in his final two operas he didn't have his final word, he still demonstrated what a privileged musician's temperament he had, and how lamentable a loss his death was to Italian art.

---

1 There is explicitly supernatural material in the source novel, *Die Geier-Wally*.

2 This is obviously not true of *La Falce* ('The Scythe').

Loreley and *La Wally* are two stages in Catalani's evolution, but their value is intrinsic and absolute; both the musically richer *Loreley* and the dramatically more effective *La Wally* will remain in the repertoire; initially neglected, they show signs of taking root and will take root ever more surely.[1] They don't sparkle like a firework that lights up in an instant, in an instant explodes and shines, and in an instant is gone; they persuade and move and insinuate their spell, little by little, with spontaneity of invention, with purity of lines, with sincerity of sentiment, with a sweetness that at the right time and place knows how to transform itself into vigour; strength and not emphasis, gold and not paste. In *Loreley*, and even better in *La Wally*, Catalani has abandoned the ancient forms and attempted, and for the most part successfully, musical drama: legendary in *Loreley*, realistic in *La Wally*.[2]

Catalani was a character; if in life he wasn't appreciated as he deserved, circumstances and his nature were to blame. 'I'm only half lucky,' he'd bitterly observe; yet somebody or other would hurl his supposedly excessive luck back in his face: see what jealousy and rivalry can do. And what did Catalani's fortune come to in the end? To this: that he had to struggle – and wait while others cut across him – so as to get his operas performed; he had to fight and make concessions to obtain the position as professor at the Conservatory; he had to fight alone and overcome the discouragement into which he was tempted by his failing health, enforced rest and people's neglect, which would enshroud him in a dark sullenness.

---

1 See below, pp. 122–24 and *Composer of Lucca*, 10–12. Depanis's prediction turned out to be both true and untrue.

2 Jay Nicolaisen offers detailed support for the claim made here, arguing that '*La Wally* … is one of a trio of operas (the others being *Falstaff* and *Manon Lescaut*), first performed within months of each other, that confirmed the advent of a vigorous new style in Italian opera. *La Wally* is not a number opera … Musically it carries forward certain techniques first noticed in *Loreley*' (158).

Catalani was never lucky with tenors, despite having tenors with good names. Barbacini, Vergnet, Mierzwinski, Ortisi, and Suagnes – either ill, or unsuitable, or less popular with the public – very nearly compromised the success of *Elda*, *Dejanice*, *Edmea* and *La Wally*.[1] By contrast, he found in Turolla, Pantaleoni, Ferni-Germano and Darclée excellent and passionate interpreters.[2] When, by sheer chance, he seemed to be about to knock the nail on the head, there you are, public attention was violently attracted somewhere else by clamorous events, and the hammer would remain hanging in mid-air.[3] To his disadvantage, Catalani couldn't push and shove; didn't know how to blow his own trumpet, put on a blustering air, cry out to the mob – admire me as I admire myself –; he disdained adulation, flattery, ostentation to the point of seeming irritable.[4] In such a way, given that the theatre world is

---

1 References to these tenors can be found in the notes above: Barbacini appeared in the first production of *Elda*, Vergnet in the first production of *Dejanice*, Mierzwinski in the Turin production of *Dejanice*, Ortisi in the first production of *Edmea*, Suagnes in the first production of *La Wally*.

2 References to these sopranos can be found in the notes above: Turolla created the role of Dejanice, Pantaleoni sang the role at Turin, Ferni-Germano created the roles of both Edmea and Loreley, Darclée the role of Wally.

3 Depanis clearly refers to a number of events here, but the overwhelming success of *Cavalleria Rusticana* just three months after the long-delayed premiere of *Loreley* is perhaps the one that best fits the description.

4 Depanis has a note here: 'When *Aida* was performed at the Paris Opera, a French composer, who had a moment of popularity in Italy, telegraphed the journalists in Milan with these words: "Aïda, succés colossal, Krauss admirable, enthousiasme public inconnu jusqu'ici. Suis bien heureux." (*Aida*, colossal success, Krauss admirable, public enthusiasm unknown before now. Am very happy). Catalani, reporting the telegram, noted: "This is what's called being cunning!" – Exactly what he was not.' The telegram was sent by Jules Massenet in 1880, and Catalani quoted it, complete with his comment, in a letter to Depanis of March that year. Letters 3. Massenet's *Le Roi de Lahore* had made a huge impact at La Scala in February 1879, playing for twenty performances.

now based on enticement, stage-management and puffs, in such a way, while alive you can't get very far; you can perhaps after your death, but that's another matter. It should be added that between 1878 and 1892 a radical change took place in the public and in the critics: Wagner was placed on every altar and Wagnerism became an idolatry. Catalani, accused of Wagneritis when Wagner was a sort of musical Antichrist, all of a sudden saw himself accused of lese-majesty when Wagner was the Word and completely infallible. Always the same story; freedom is cried up everywhere, it's no to conventional formulas, down with the chains that hamper genius, – and then one formula is replaced with another, new chains take the place of the old, and it's ahead, *marche*, in the name of liberty, lined up in the same file, all in the shadow of the same banner. Catalani was an enthusiastic admirer of Wagner, but thought that the artist must think with his own and not another's head, even if it were the head of the greatest musical genius. That was right thinking, and while he despised submitting to the Wagnerian yoke, Catalani would burn with saintly rage every time he heard or read ill-considered and irreverent judgments upon Wagner. An extravagant telegram from Berlin, published in most of the newspapers, boasting that the new Italian school had marginalized Wagner's works in Germany, had the virtue of making him lose his temper: 'I'm glad,' he wrote, 'not to be considered among those who have so much responsibility!!! Lucky them if their shoulders are so solid as to accept Wagner's legacy!'[1]

---

[1] Letter of 20 May 1893. Letters 133–34. Immediately before the passage that Depanis quotes, Catalani had asked: 'Did you see the telegram from Berlin in yesterday's *Corriere della sera*, where it is said that Wagner has been completely abandoned in German theatres and replaced by Mascagni, Leoncavallo, Puccini and Franchetti?' (133). Catalani was no doubt particularly hurt not to be on the list, as *La Wally* had been performed in Hamburg in February 1893 to considerable acclaim. On 28 February Catalani reported to Depanis that the impresario Bernhard Pollini had 'assured' him that '*La Wally* was the biggest success [in Germany] among the works imported from Italy.' Letters 129.

Alfredo Catalani wasn't handsome, he was *simpatico*,[1] and he enjoyed much sympathy in the world of women: the double halo of genius and illness attracts the heart of a woman whose love borders on pity. He was extremely cultured, with a wide intellectual outlook, but ill-provided in the practical sense of life; in this he was a child with an ingenuousness only exceeded by his absentmindedness: and between the two he was given some bad turns. For Turin and Piedmont he nourished an affection that was never denied; Turin was for him a second homeland, and he would call Piedmont 'his own beloved Piedmont.'[2] 'Here in Allevard,' he proudly recorded in 1887, 'there are various Turin people, and what's more, the ladies from Turin hold the record for beauty and elegance.'[3] And he would never miss an opportunity to visit Turin and Piedmont and to celebrate the inhabitants' courtesy and the places' beauty. 'I'm enchanted by this part of Piedmont too!' he wrote from Mondovì where he was Signora Bendazzi's guest, 'Long live the Piedmont!'[4] These were private exclamations, not calculated telegrams, thus sincere. In his character he had a level of witty joviality unknown to most, for Catalani didn't reveal himself too much beyond his

---

[1] Depanis has a note here: 'Catalani had an essentially romantic look. Tranquillo Cremona portrayed him in his painting, *L'Edera* (The Ivy), which belongs to Benedetto Junck, Catalani's friend and companion from the Conservatory; another oil portrait, maybe the sketch that was used for the painting, is owned by Count Franchi. And I have the gesso head by Troubetzkoy, full of expression, shown three years ago at the *Permanente* in Milan.' Cremona's picture has been reproduced in most books on the composer, including *Composer of Lucca*, and can be readily found on the internet. The painting was made in 1878, when Catalani was still in relatively good heath. Count Franchi is Ippolito Valletta, for whom see above, p. 45 n. 3. The head by Paul Troubetzkoy (1866–1938) was made in 1890. A photograph of it was published by Carlo Gatti in his 1953 biography of Catalani, *Catalani: La Vita e le Opere*, plate after p. 240.

[2] There is a similar expression in a letter of 16 July 1891. Letters 88.

[3] Letter of 11 July 1887. Letters 43.

[4] Letter of 20 September 1889. Letters 67.

narrow circle of friends and also because joviality didn't find a suitable terrain for expression in that body gnawed by illness.

In these last years his hair became grey, his eye-sockets more sunken, his cheeks more bony, his figure more curved. He wouldn't spend time complaining, but rather made an effort to seem cheerful in the reckless hope of deluding both himself and others, and would talk and laugh with a shrill, nervous, sobbing laugh. Suddenly his laugh would die on his lips, the morbid redness of excitement in his cheeks would disappear, and he would interrupt what he was saying and stare ahead, his eyes abstracted, blank: what visions, what mysteries slid by in those eyes!

Catalani suffered intensely from a remorseless illness that strikes at the spirit through the body; his correspondence is an endless succession of hopes and fears, a continuous oscillation of pitiful illusions and lucid, disturbing intervals. 'I am in a terrible mood,' he writes in June 1884, 'because the doctor wants me to stop working for a couple of months. Such fun, living!'[1] A little later: 'The symphonic poem progresses but slowly because my stomach won't let me work.'[2] In the summer he experiences an improvement thanks to a treatment begun at Gais: 'I've started my treatment and I find it good. Here the air is excellent. Gais is at about a thousand metres elevation in the middle of meadows and forests of firs. Will I manage to put on a little weight?'[3]

In August 1885 Catalani goes to Masino in Valtellina and releases a hymn to health: 'I can't tell you how much this pure, balsamic air, impregnated with the scent of firs and pines, has done me good. In no time at all I've been really transformed. *This consoles me, because it proves I don't have serious internal trouble.*'[4]

---

1 Letter of 10 June 1884. Letters 13.
2 Letter of 19 June 1884. Letters 14.
3 Letter of 12 July 1884. Letters 14.
4 Letter of 16 August 1885. Letters 20.

Oh, unhappy soul! – In July 1886 he heads for Levico, from where he plans to depart 'perfectly *good as new*. These arsenic and ferruginous baths are truly miraculous.'[1] In fact in October, during the rehearsals of *Edmea* at the Carignano, he coughs up a mouthful of blood, and another in April 1887, and it prevents him from coming to Tuscany for the rehearsal of his symphonic poem *Ero e Leandro*. The news is received and exaggerated by the newspapers, and he is concerned not to be believed either consumptive, or finished, and writes from Florence: 'My health is fair as ever. The rumour that I'm *very seriously* (!) ill has spread so much that letters rain down on me from every side. Any newspaper that would care to report that I'm well and I'm in Florence would be performing an act of charity.'[2] Catalani was twice in Allevard in Savoy, the first time with good results, the second with less.[3] In winter he used to spend some time on the Riviera, depending on the degree of freedom allowed him by his teaching duties, and it's one of these 'escapes' to the country of sunshine to which the following passage from a letter of 3 March 1890 refers, breathing an unusual festive air: 'Only on my arrival in San Remo was I persuaded that I really had settled to come here. I exclaimed: am I actually here? in the country of palm trees? And now that I'm here I don't regret it, because if yesterday was critical, today there shines the finest spring sun one can imagine, and everywhere there's the scent of violets and blossoming orange-trees! – This morning I was strolling along an avenue all palms and olives, thinking about how to find my friend Melano, when at the turning of a path I heard singing, in a voice that wasn't Ferni's: "tu sei qui?" (what, you here?)' (the start of the love duet in *Edmea*). 'It was indeed him, my friend Melano, who was coming towards me ...' My friend Melano,

---

1 Letter of 19 July 1886. Letters 26.
2 Letter of 5 May 1887. Letters 40.
3 In the summers of 1887 and 1888.

another of the dear, lamented dead.[1] I'm taking a turn in a cemetery of people and memories!

As if consumption were not enough, there were added intestinal troubles, rheumatic pains, and a disease of the ear that proved resistant to any cure: 'My ear continues to torment me with such neuralgic pain that I'm going out of my head,' he wrote in August 1890. 'Now I'm here in Faido, among the mountains, trying to get my strength up a bit, and to become a little fatter, if possible. For me that's a more arduous task than writing an opera.'[2] For a whole year he attended the hospital of the Fatebenefratelli in Milan,[3] queuing patiently with the other sick people and waiting his turn; the level and acuteness of the pains lessened, but the ear didn't heal. Having begun to doubt that the Milanese climate was propitious for him, he was considering a change of residence: 'I would be glad to go, sure that I'll gain in health and in artistic terms, because *mens sana in corpore sano*, and I would work both more and better.'[4] But he would have had to leave the Conservatory and, unless a similar post elsewhere came to his aid, the condition of his finances did not allow him to renounce his three thousand lira salary. So he made do with a series of other projects: a Mediterranean cruise, a winter journey to the Indies, for which he would have requested a temporary leave

---

[1] Melano apparently died in early 1892. Catalani wrote to Depanis on 19 January: 'You can't imagine the sad feeling that I experienced at the news of the death of Commendatore Melano, whom I loved with a sincere and felt friendship!' Letters 97. The suggestion seems to be that Melano, like Catalani, was an invalid.

[2] Letter of 3 August 1890 (the letter Depanis prints in facsimile in his later memoir). Letters 81.

[3] A traditional religious hospital founded by Carlo Borromeo (1538–84), Archbishop of Milan, and administered by the Brothers Hospitallers of St. John of God.

[4] Letter of 21 October 1889. Letters 68. The well-known Latin phrase (from Juvenal) means 'a healthy mind in a healthy body.'

for reasons of health. At first seasickness frightened him; then, as a result of a crossing between Palermo and Naples, he felt reassured and would boast of being 'bomb-proof, ready to make a round-the-world tour.'[1] In a final postcard of 19 July this year he was still talking to me of a month on a sailing ship in order to refortify his lungs with the salt sea air.[2]

Man proposes and God disposes. Catalani wasn't warmed by the sun in the Indies, he didn't breathe the strong sea breezes, nor did he set sail for his world tour, – he crossed its borders to rest his tired soul in the endless calm of eternity.

If I have commemorated the man more than the artist, and if I have lingered on a series of troubles and sorrows, compassionate souls will understand and make allowances for me. To speak of the maestro I would have pummelled my brains, to speak of my friend the heart was enough. I have listened to the voice of the heart, and from the heart of the reader I beg a little love for poor Alfredo.

Writing about him, a wave of memories overwhelms me, and I almost see his pale figure; it seems to me that his sorrowful eyes glance at these papers of mine and his colourless lips break into a gentle smile. I extend my hand to shake his, but no, it is an illusion, and I find only his letters spread on the table, documents from the past, and one among them stands out, the one in which he announces to me the future opera that death truncated, *Nella Selva*.[3] Then I raise my eyes. The sky has an immaculate serenity in which the gaze plunges as in an azure dome: in the afternoon atmosphere there is a vertiginous vibration of atoms; the hills quiver as they extend all around, soft and verdant; the mountains quiver on the extreme horizon beyond

---

1 Letter of 26 January 1893. Letters 127.
2 Letters 139.
3 The letter of 20 June 1893. Letters 136.

the misty plain, it too quivering. The torrent's grumble arises from the valley, from above comes the birds' twittering and a vague peal of bells, confused, mysteriously echoing in the air. In the infinite brightness nature sleeps, and the artist sleeps, he who would have wanted to snatch from it the secret of its poetry, to transfuse it into a song, drawing the colour from the radiance of the sky and the feeling from the intimate voices of things. And I think of the friend constrained between four small planks, under the soil, where there is no light, where there is no sound, – of the friend that I could not see again and could not kiss one last time on the forehead, and that I will never see any more, will not kiss ever again …

Sassi Torinese, 13–16 August 1893

Appendix: Adapting Elda as Loreley[1]

THE CHANGES Catalani made to *Elda* are substantial. *Elda* was in four acts and nine scenes; of these, the second in Act One, the second and third in Act Two, the third in Act Three and the first in Act Four were eliminated; the four acts were reduced to three, and the remaining scenes rearranged from start to finish in the libretto and in the music with relevant additions and transpositions. Thus the chorus of fishermen from the second scene of Act One in *Elda* became the party chorus in the second part of Act Two in *Loreley*; the nuptial march theme in the second part of *Elda*, 'Caro fior di queste sponde' (Dear flower of these banks), and the one for the chorus from the third part of Act Two, 'Dea del Walhalla' (Goddess of Valhalla), served as a basis for the epithalamium in *Loreley*; the tenor's romanza from *Elda* was transformed into the little duet between Walter and Anna in Act Two of *Loreley*; the theme 'Maligno spirto che il gaudio uccidi'

---

[1] As noted above, this was originally attached to footnote 1 on p. 88.

(Malignant spirit who murders mirth) from the third scene in Act Two of *Elda* was introduced into the prelude of *Loreley* and returns in the second finale, 'Oh! incanto irresistibile!' (Oh! irresistible enchantment!); the 'stretta' of the third finale from *Elda* is glimpsed in the curses of the chorus interrupting the funeral march in *Loreley*. The second part of Act Two of *Loreley* consists of situations removed from the finales of Acts One and Two of *Elda*. The Dance of the Ondines, with minimal rearrangements to the music, moved from the first scene of Act Two of *Elda* to Act Three of *Loreley*, and the waltzer[1] from the second scene in Act One passed to the second part of Act Two. The pieces from *Elda* that retain their fundamental structure in *Loreley* are the prelude, the duet between Walter and Loreley, the evocation, the waltzer, the funeral march, the Dance of the Ondines, and the final duet.

---

1 The 'Valzer dei Fiori,' or 'Waltz of Flowers.'

Giovanni Depanis (1823–89)

Alfredo Catalani: A Later Memoir[1]

Giuseppe Depanis

[Originally published in 1915 in the second volume of *I Concerti Popolari ed il Teatro Regio di Torino*, pp. 69–87.]

ALFREDO CATALANI'S *Elda* was looked forward to with a certain curiosity, not so much by the Regio's regular audience, for whom the maestro was a nobody, as by the Milanese musical world. They recalled the hopes stirred by *La Falce*, performed in July 1875 in the little theatre of the Milan Conservatory as Catalani's diploma piece. Ernest Reyer had confessed that no young French composer would have been capable of performing so well in a first work, and the austere Società del Quartetto conceded to *La Falce* the truly exceptional honour of producing it again in one of their concerts, usually inaccessible for debuting composers.[2]

I met Catalani in 1878. Furnished with a letter of recommendation from Signora Lucca, and accompanied by Ippolito Valletta, the maestro came to Turin to present the opera he had ready for staging to the examination of Carlo Pedrotti

---

1 Parts of this repeat material, though often with interesting variations, from the 1893 account. This material is not separately annotated here.

2 It was in fact just the overture to *La Falce* that the Società performed, as Depanis makes clear in his earlier biography.

and my father. He wished to submit his work to the judgment of a Turin public undisturbed by the competition between publishers and the insidiousness of fellow composers. Similar proposals often arrived, encouraged by the rumour that the Regio was the Mecca for maestros looking for a theatre to stage their offspring. We had to put up with all sorts of things, and our sorry experiences had made us sceptical and resigned to the worst.

Catalani's appearance was distinctly in his favour. Slim, pale, slender; his forehead high; his nose aquiline; his moustache drooping; his copious hair somewhat curling; his eyes clear and deep under thick protruding eyebrows. He walked with a slight stoop; was gentle, timid, detached; he rarely laughed, with an almost convulsive laugh; would speak softly, and punctuated his words with little fits of coughing. He was young, barely twenty-four; and looked even younger thanks to the ingenuousness of his manners and his frail physique. 'He's catching his soul in his teeth,' said the wife of Cichin the custodian, filled with pity for him, and with its colloquial effectiveness her exclamation hit the nail on the head.

The sheer bulk of the score Catalani placed on the music rack of the piano wrecked the excellent impression given by the man: four acts, four tall, thick manuscript volumes. Carlo D'Ormeville had transferred the legend of the Loreley from the Rhine to the Baltic and constructed upon it nine scenes of good verse and good situation, but prolix and confused; at any rate, it was a libretto more suitable for an experienced artist than for a beginner. Pedrotti asked Catalani how he had dared tackle such a difficult libretto, and Catalani seemed astonished, surprised by the question and unaware of any difficulty. He sat at the piano and began the audition. He was an outstanding pianist, but afflicted with a cracked, caprine voice: and he wasn't willing to play without accompanying the music with song. Pedrotti puffed impatiently and would invite him to be quiet; all to no avail, a few minutes later the cracked voice was spoiling the piano performance again.

There followed, thanks to the score's exuberance and beauty, three hours of pleasure and pain. 'There's enough music here for two operas!' cried Pedrotti between enthusiasm and irritation, and Catalani with staring eyes was unsure in his turn if he ought to be rejoicing or feeling upset. My father had developed a sympathy for Catalani and promised to perform the opera provided the maestro lightened some passages, rearranged others, and employed the scissors with gusto through the four large volumes. Catalani accepted, and took on the task of preparing a shortened and simplified score by the Carnival of 1880. He kept his promise and made extensive changes and cuts, although that blessed Baltic Spirit appeared no less overburdened. Everyone grumbled at the rehearsals; the exigencies of staging have to be respected and writing some good music isn't enough; moreover, one has to keep in mind the artists, the suppliers, the stagehands. With indomitable courage Pedrotti completed what the maestro had begun and kept cutting mercilessly; at first Catalani, tormented in his paternal loins, showed signs of protesting, then resigned himself to the inevitable. The rehearsals for *Elda* were forever famous in the annals of the Regio, the cuts mounted up to eighteen, and little by little another quarter of the score disappeared after a first quarter had already been sacrificed by the author in his rearrangement. When the sting of the wound passed, Catalani was forever grateful to Pedrotti for the healthy lesson.

Elda saw the stage lights on the evening of Saturday 31 January 1880. Under the direction of Pedrotti, its godparents were Edouard De Reszke (King of Leira), Nadina Bulicioff (Ulla), Enrico Barbacini (Sveno), Adele Garbini (Elda), and Sante Athos (Magno); a group of artists such as a beginner rarely chances on, a genuine stroke of luck, as the envious murmured, accusing Catalani of this and more, so much does music refine conduct. Luck, yes, perhaps, partial luck. On the very day of the first performance both Bulicioff and Barbacini fell ill; being only slight, Bulicioff's indisposition didn't prevent her from singing; Barbacini's case was more serious. Postponement would have been disastrous; of the many people from Milan hurrying to attend the young maestro's debut, not all nurtured within the sympathy they professed aloud and postponement would have produced the comments of which only those familiar with the theatre world can judge the seriousness. At the crossroads between a postponement with its backbiting aftermath and a performance amputated by Barbacini's illness and Bulicioff's indisposition, publisher, maestro and impresario chose performance and ruled out postponement. Barbacini, in a spirit of self-denial, sacrificed himself for the maestro. But the trouble didn't end here. The harpist Pinto – may he rest in peace as a good man and excellent harpist – was about to take his seat in the orchestra when he announced to Pedrotti that he was feeling ill, would do his best, but feared himself unable to bear the strain. Now Catalani, who always had a special predilection for the harp, from which he drew singularly poetic effects, had, in the first version of *Elda*, even overdone it, and in addition, as the structure of the Regio orchestra included only one harp, the harpist was expected to relocate more than once from orchestra to stage so as to accompany incidental songs and choruses, and then return to the orchestra. A few evenings previously, at one of the performances of *Poliuto*,[1] Pinto had already been struck by a sudden malady, and the clarinets had there and then to replace the angelic harps; but the expedient wouldn't work for *Elda*. And so? Trust in God and get along with an ill tenor, an indisposed prima donna, and a harpist in a weak state of health. 'Complete madness, this,' Pedrotti grumbled, slumping his shoulders and counting off a rosary of typically

---

1 Donizetti's opera, written in 1838 and first performed in 1848.

Veronese exclamations. – I had a bottle of *vin generoso* brought to the rehearsal room next to the stage, called 'the comforter' because that's where the maestros used to await their sentence; and giving sips to Pinto during the intervals between his peregrinations, and sips to Catalani, pale and skinny, I was busy the whole evening stimulating the timid and supporting the infirm; my father did the rest for Barbacini. When the curtain came down on the final scene of the final act, we all heaved a sigh of relief; the nightmare was over.

The reception given the opera was excellent in the first act and in the first part of the second, cooled in the second half of the second and the third act, improved again in the fourth, where a heroic effort by Barbacini overcame the hoarseness that troubled him, and three curtain calls greeted Catalani and the artists at the end of the opera. In essence, it was a victory achieved in difficult circumstances. Barbacini having got worse, the second performance was postponed to the following Saturday, 7 February; twenty curtain calls and an encore for the tenor's romanza confirmed the happy success of the first night. The success though was more the maestro's than the opera's, an act of hope if not faith, and during the nine performances a handful of small troubles revealed the sullen attitude of a group, few in truth, of season-ticket holders. From some of the small boxes in the third row, the same ones that would howl down *Carmen* and *Melusina*[1] the following year, hisses emerged, soon drowned out by the applause, hisses not so much addressed to the opera as calling for a change of programme: *Elda* was only on its seventh performance. As chance would have it at that very moment Catalani was passing along the corridor, right next to the small boxes of those hissing. It was as if he'd been stabbed to the heart. 'What have I done to them?' he exclaimed as a tear

---

1 The now forgotten *Melusine* (1875) by the German composer Karl Grammann (1842–97).

sprang out upon his eyelashes, and he ran off almost as if chased by a pack of hounds barking at his heels.

After Turin, *Elda* migrated to Warsaw. Then it slept the sleep of the just on the publisher's shelves. The impresarios were not wrong: the opera in its primitive form contained buds of vitality, but one couldn't call it a vital organism. Catalani became persuaded of this himself, and was already contemplating recasting it from top to bottom, but first he wanted to attempt the stage again with *Dejanice* and *Edmea* so as not to be called incapable of creating and constrained to live on his own left-overs. Only after *Edmea*, his least original opera but the one which during his lifetime provided him with his greatest triumphs, did he set himself again to *Elda*, stripping it of the beggar's clothes which had made Loreley into a Baltic Fairy, and giving back to the legend its real meaning. Far too many surgeons worked on the rearrangement, and because of the collaboration of an excessive number of people the rather unintegrated second act suffered in particular.[1] On the whole, however, the libretto for *Loreley* is distinctly more concise and effective than that for *Elda* and would even make a good romantic libretto were it not for the unfortunate creation of Hermann that must weigh on the conscience of the poet Zanardini. In all this confusion the entire funeral march came very near to being suppressed because 'although beautiful, all funeral marches have always had the effect of being fire extinguishers,' argued Zanardini, and Catalani, influenced by his desire to disprove those critics reproaching him for indulging in

---

[1] Depanis himself was one of the surgeons, and established the main principles of the revision: see *Lettere di Alfredo Catalani e Giuseppe Depanis*, ed. Carlo Gatti (Milan, 1946), 28–30. Most of the detailed rewriting was entrusted to Angelo Zanardini (1820–93), who had earlier written *Dejanice* for Catalani: his name appears on the libretto and score, along with that of Carlo D'Ormeville, the writer of *Elda*. D'Ormeville himself seems to have had a hand in the revisions, Catalani, too, was actively involved, and in the later stages Luigi Illica and Giuseppe Giacosa made contributions.

minor modalities, almost consented.[1] Fortunately I managed to prevent such a vandalizing suppression.

In November 1887 Catalani wrote to me: 'I am persuaded that *Loreley*, redone in this way, will become a fairy deserving of respect, so long as she's willing to travel in search of money for her papa.' He rested a good deal of his hopes on *Loreley*: 'it's my best work,' he'd repeat, 'and it will be a hundred times superior to *Edmea*, which I'm getting tired of.'[2] Two years were needed for *Loreley* to find a theatre from which to embark on the desired journey in search of money for its father, even though the author was no longer a beginner and *Edmea* had gained him a respectable popularity. The theatre was again the Regio in Turin.

The comparison between the old *Elda* and the new *Loreley* on the same stage that had witnessed the birth of *Elda* promised to be interesting; however the season-ticket holders and some of the impresarios (given that in 1889 the theatre was managed by a Society of a hundred gentlemen: so many brains, so many ideas) began to complain that the opera was not completely new. And once again a series of troubles hampered *Loreley*'s rehearsals as they had those for *Elda* – Catalani's so-called luck!: – the death of my father, the Society's director, the 'influenza' which raged among the artists and the ranks of chorus and orchestra, the mourning after Prince Amadeo's death – and again on the eve

---

1 Catalani had written to Depanis on 4 July 1887: 'Zanardini would gladly sacrifice the whole funeral march because, no matter how beautiful it is, all funeral marches have always had the effect, according to him, of being "fire-extinguishers." And perhaps he isn't wrong.' Letters 42. By 11 July Depanis had apparently convinced Catalani that the funeral march should stay: Letters 43. Most subsequent critics have considered it one of the highlights of the score.

2 The claim (expressed in a letter of 22 February 1887) had in fact been that *Loreley* would be 'twenty times' superior. Depanis quotes the passage correctly in his earlier account: see above, p. 81. Of course Catalani may have made larger claims in conversation.

of performance the tenor Durot's falling ill. The dress rehearsal without the tenor took place behind closed doors, provoking protests from the hundred impresarios and the artists' families, who, when it comes to rehearsals, acquire a frightening elasticity and create around the score an atmosphere of mistrust.

Directed by Edoardo Mascheroni and performed by Virginia Ferni-Germano (a marvellous Loreley), by Natale Pozzi (Rodolfo), by Eleonora Dexter (Anna), by Eugenio Durot (Walter), by Enrico Stinco-Palermini (Hermann), the opera at last overcame the obstacles placed in its way by bad luck and made its debut on 17 February 1890, the Sunday before Carnival, to a distracted and moody audience.[1] A tacit hostility snaking among the seats and in the boxes found no way of expressing itself; the first act was welcomed with unanimous applause, the second passed in silence, the third achieved the same success as the first, which four final curtain calls put a seal on. Catalani didn't want to appear on stage with the curtain up; his example, which deserved praise, instead provided a weapon for his adversaries – of which he had many in the artistic world, again chorusing how music mitigates behaviour – who spread to the four winds the news that there had been less than ten curtain calls and that, according to a metric measure, the opera had been a fiasco. The following performances proved these barely charitable predictions wrong, and once even the second act became better appreciated, *Loreley*, together with *Lohengrin*, proved the life-support for a miserably poor season.

Loreley and *La Wally* remain to demonstrate how exquisite an artist Catalani was, and what he could have given us had death not struck him down at the height of his maturation. They are certainly not perfect operas, but Catalani renders attractive even their partial imperfections because he disdains

---

1 Again Depanis gets the date wrong: it was actually 16 February.

the artifice of seeming and not being; always sincere, he sings as he feels without swelling his voice to deceive the audience about himself. For recompense, what frequent purity of lines, what spontaneity of invention, what distinguished form, what elegant episodes! In the maestro's music there is something of the landscape of his native Tuscany, with its pellucid horizons. And Catalani knows how to suggest his vision of it without straying from the musical field, and without giving way to the exaggerations of descriptive music.

In fifteen years, alternating periods of feverish work with enforced rest, Catalani created *La Falce, Elda, Dejanice, Edmea, Loreley, La Wally*, to mention only his works for the theatre, and to say nothing of the minor compositions. All his operas have a female name as their title;[1] he was *par excellence* a singer of women, and to express the eternal feminine he had tender notes similar to kisses, exquisite sweetnesses similar to caresses. *Elda* signals the beginning of the young Italian school (*giovane scuola*). When Giacomo Puccini's *Le Villi* was performed in Hamburg, critics noted the points of contact with *Cavalleria Rusticana*, forgetting that the opera by Mascagni postdates the opera by Puccini; *Le Villi* is even more of a piece with *Elda*. If Catalani was the first to be successful we are obliged to acknowledge that he is the initiator of the school that derives from him. Puccini and Mascagni have reaped so much applause as to pride themselves on being Tuscan, and they bring a double glory to the region. *Dejanice* carries within itself an incurable original vice – the libretto, a mixture of situations from *L'Africana*, *Aida* and *La Gioconda*, diluted in a Greek sauce, which is a pity because it contains precious passages: the nostalgic monologue of Labdaco, the duet between Dejanice and Argelia, the chorus of the hetaerae, and the whole fourth act of immense and painful dramatic strength. *Edmea* is the

---

[1] This is obviously not true of *La Falce*.

demonstration of a crisis, and Catalani thought too well of himself not to rebel against the destiny of going down in history only as the author of this opera, for he recognized that a good half of *Edmea*'s success was thanks to his prima donna, Virginia Ferni-Germano. With *La Wally* Catalani decisively affirms what had been wrongly contested: that he has the temper of an opera composer. Though in the matter of invention it may be inferior to *Loreley*, from the dramatic and theatrical point of view *La Wally* is a more organic work. If we discount the ballad in the first act and the quartet in the second, the composer isn't loitering along the way; he advances promptly towards the target, at times even with excessive haste, when we're moved to regret that he forces the music with such rigour into the bottleneck of the drama.

I have mentioned Catalani's talent for invention and colour. I could give many more examples, but it is enough for me merely to recall the Dance of the Ondines and the funeral march in *Loreley*, the first finale and the fourth prelude in *La Wally*.

The Dance of the Ondines combines the poetic appeal of the invention with the elegance of the instrumental embroidery. The soft melody murmured by the muted strings, and taken up with great inventiveness by the trumpet as a distant echo, accompanies the voluptuous movements of the Ondines under the pale moon's rays, and the musical vision is so complete that the reality of the representation offends us and we prefer to close our eyes, to abandon ourselves to the seduction of the dream.

Anna's funeral march: oh! how sad and disconsolate in its simplicity! Without emphasis, a lament that stirs the heart and moistens the eyelids, a deep desperate sigh without relief, without pause. The procession flows into the forest amidst the glimmers from the candles and the last twilight gleams; it disappears; the voices weaken, fall silent, and yet there lingers in the air the resonance of the disconsolate lullaby and those few notes we cannot forget; it's something of us lost forever, it's our youth:

Why, oh why did you depart,
Why did you leave us with such pain?
Away from life, oh why
Did you spread your flight to the sky?

The Act One finale in *La Wally* arouses no less emotion when the girl climbs the tiring slope of the mountain, listens to the echo of the pious bell, and looks towards the earth as if towards a memory. Twilight draws on, the Ave Maria tolls. The pious old ladies whisper a prayer. The ineffable evening peace hangs over us and in this peace we too would like to pass up there through the white snow where neither regret nor pain exists ...

And a vision of the high mountain, of the glacier's desolate immensity, leaps from the fourth act prelude, superb for the nobility of its ideas, for the austerity of its construction, for the efficacy of the instrumentation. Turbid thoughts distress Wally's mind. She no longer has a family. Her mother has died, her father has driven her away, she's been deceived by her lover. For an instant she seems to hear, carried on the wind's wings, the yodeler from the Sölden Fair, but soon a dreadful delusion seizes her mind before shame makes her leap to her feet on the point of blaspheming.[1] But no. An infinite and resigned melancholy descends upon her. The nature surrounding her is dead: white flowers of snow, white tumuli of snow, white distances of snow. Soon she too will dissolve into the immense whiteness. Music has been defined as the art of expressing with sound the spirit of what could otherwise barely be signified. It's true. No picture and no poetry would be able to reach the expressive height of this musical passage.

---

[1] Depanis's explanation here is rather curious. Though he is apparently describing simply the prelude he effectively glosses it with a not particularly accurate account of what happens several pages later when Wally first hears Walter's 'jodling song' drifting up the mountainside and then the sounds of Hagenbach approaching. Walter had previously sung the song at Hochstoff, however, not the Sölden Fair.

In spite of possessing similar beauties, *Loreley* and *La Wally* encountered obstacles in making their way. *Loreley* was repeated at Genoa, Rome and Palermo; *La Wally* was played in Milan, Lucca, Genoa and Hamburg. When Catalani died in 1893, both *La Wally*, staged in Turin, and *Loreley*, in Milan and Trieste, in homage to the deceased composer, achieved only lukewarm success. Reading the newspapers of that time is very revealing indeed. Through the superficial benevolence there seeps out the conviction that Catalani's operas have died, along with their author, and *Loreley*'s music is declared by most to be of limited inventiveness and dull in colour. Very few had faith in *Loreley*'s and *La Wally*'s vitality, and among those few were G. B. Nappi of the *Perseveranza* and the present writer.[1] For a few years not a word was spoken of Catalani, *verismo* was raging, and the poor Ondines were not at ease among the many murders that had transformed operatic theatre into a branch of the Crown Court. A first attempt at exhumation, with Leopoldo Mugnone as promoter, saw *La Wally* fail at the Costanzi in Rome, for the times were not ripe and the surroundings unsuitable.[2] The honour and merit of awakening *Loreley* and *La Wally* from their long sleep and of avenging them before public and critics rests with Arturo Toscanini, who had begun his career as a conductor with Catalani in Turin and who attended upon Catalani's last breath.[3]

---

[1] Giovanni Battista Nappi (1857–1932), an important and influential critic whose 1918 biographical article on Catalani is included in *Composer of Lucca*.

[2] Leopoldo Mugnone (1858–1941), an important conductor who also composed operas in the *verismo* style. He was the resident conductor at the Teatro Costanzi, where he famously conducted the first performances of *Cavalleria Rusticana* in 1890. He revived *La Wally* there in December 1899.

[3] As John W. Klein argued, 'the turning of the tide' in Catalani's stage fortunes occurred when Toscanini conducted *La Wally* with great success in Buenos Aires in summer 1904. See 'Toscanini and Catalani – A Unique Friendship,' *Music and Letters* 48 (1967), 226.

Arturo Toscanini, 1904

In 1904, the year he restored *La Wally* to the modern repertoire, Toscanini signed this photograph on what would have been Catalani's 50th birthday.

There was general astonishment, almost as if audiences and critics suddenly found themselves in the presence of persons unfairly neglected but not entirely forgotten thanks to friends in common who had adopted their habits and way of dressing. *Loreley* and *La Wally* have now established themselves as part of the contemporary operatic repertoire.[1] But Alfredo Catalani is dead.

This is a typical case. The maestros are legion who, having been praised to the skies, then disappear from the scene even before their own disappearance. Catalani, on the contrary, does not disappoint hopes, each stage on his journey marks a step towards an ideal of nobility, he introduces forms and procedures that later had good fortune, being taken to the maximum of expressiveness by vigorous talents or merely disfigured by mediocre ones. And yet those he had encouraged, or those who came upon his heels, triumphed, while he remained in the second division, cut off from the mainstream. Then we witnessed a fact even more marvellous, which is that, while for many death is a synonym of oblivion, for Catalani it was synonymous with resurrection. The causes for such a phenomenon are various, not easy to explain, and even less to comprehend for those who did not live through Catalani's times. The subject is delicate. I'm lightly touching on the matter so as to shed light on the figure of the maestro, not out of prejudice towards anyone or anything, and having learned from experience that often men, rather than creating, undergo events.

For the sake of truth I will start by saying that many of the causes can be traced to Catalani himself and his nature as an artist. These include the choice of libretto, an occasional negligence in the orchestration, the almost mincing refinement of some episodes, the insistence on certain details, derived from his

---

[1] Between 1904 and 1915 there had been dozens of productions of both operas, all listed on Roberto Marcocci's very useful website, <http://www.lavoceantica.it/Cronologie.htm>.

studies in France, and the tendency to sentimental indulgences and elegy. But we shouldn't exaggerate either. Negligence, or better the affecting of negligence here and there, doesn't exclude the fact that most of the time he is gentleman-like, and that in the orchestration, above all in a certain embroidery of the minor instruments, and in his way of treating the harp and the trumpet in the pianissimo passages, he has established a school in Italy. If at times he seemed to neglect the orchestration, that derived from the fact that, protective of the linear purity, he sacrificed effect for fear of falling into pompousness. Finally, the tendency to elegy and to minor tones is less marked than usually asserted. Undeniably his poor health helped to transfuse into Catalani's music a sense of melancholy not without its fascination. Yet it's still true that his languishing body prompted the argument about the languor of the music; we're made in such a way that we allow ourselves to be seduced by aprioristic deductions, turning them into exaggerated consequences.

Catalani suffered the consequences of the circumstances within which he carried out his activity. Over the previous thirty years, Italian operatic theatre had undergone a deep crisis.[1] The Wagnerian battle was raging. The public didn't know which way to turn, groped uncertainly among the various schools, and muddled together maestros and operas of opposed tendencies and values, with identical admiration and identical horror. Amidst so many contradictions they were driven to mistrust novelty, and mistook for Wagnerian derivatives even those works that were at the very opposite pole to Wagnerian art. Because of

---

1 Depanis's 'thirty years' is remarkably precise if he is understood as counting back from 1893. Two operas by the young Franco Faccio (1840–91), *I Profughi Fiamminghi* (1863) and *Amleto* (1865) had been the first to challenge Italian conventions with ultramontane influences; both had encountered opposition from traditionalists who saw in Faccio's innovations the imprint of 'the music of the future.' Faccio later became an important supporter of Catalani.

the very limited awareness the audiences then had of Wagner's music (remember how *Tannhaüser* and *Lohengrin* inspired the most ferocious conflicts![1]), to him they attributed everything, good or bad, that broke with the conventions they knew and required a slight effort of sympathetic attention. The critics had lost their bearings no more and no less than the public; divided into two opposite camps, they allowed no middle way: you were either for Wagner or against him. For the anti-Wagnerians, who covered their stubborn blindness with the veil of Italianism, Wagner was the subverter of taste, the Antichrist, to be booted out of the way; they regarded him as a barbaric accumulator of numbers without inspiration, without melody, just a mass of notes, a heap of dissonances. Their attitude was: death to Wagner and the impostors who feign admiration, that is to all the Wagnerians since sincerity of admiration was ruled out *a priori* in those of healthy intellect. For their part, the Wagnerians were not joking; beyond Wagner there was nowhere to go, the critics accepted imitators, insisted on imitation. To make anyone hear amid this pandemonium it was necessary to cry out clear and strong, to deepen your voice, violate the public, go beyond the mark. The racket was such that the appearance of *Falstaff,* the youthful development of a venerable old man, didn't suffice to quieten it.[2]

Imagine Catalani, so refined, so straightforward, so delicate! If there were deluded composers, convinced they could defeat

---

1 Depanis's point is that even these early Wagner works (first performed in Italy in 1872 and 1871 respectively) incited opposition. None of the mature music dramas were heard in Italy until 1883.

2 Verdi's *Falstaff* was premiered at La Scala on 9 February 1893. Discussing the opera's critical reception, Julian Budden writes: 'It was never to become a popular favourite. Even at the triumphal first night it was possible to discern through "the roaring and the wreaths" a certain puzzled disappointment among the public' (*The Operas of Verdi 3: From* Don Carlos *to* Falstaff [London and New York, 1981], 440).

Wagner by opposing him with their own operas, Catalani didn't feel up to such a task, as he'd exclaim with pointed irony; between presumptuous demolition and servile, monkey-like copying, he preferred to evade both and remain above all else sincere. One must lack any aesthetic criterion not to recognize that Wagner's marvellous technique is innate with his genius and with his particular perception of the lyric drama. Studying it is indispensable; but to apply it without the procedures and submit one's own way of feeling to somebody else's way of feeling, thus falsifying one's artistic impulse, is to betray the audacious spirit of freedom that sustains Wagner's reform; one kind of conventionalism is simply replaced by another. But in the struggle the passions confuse the exact vision of things. Thus Catalani saw himself neglected by a public who demanded from him what he neither wanted to give, nor could give; he was targeted by critics, both Wagnerians and anti-Wagnerians, who accused him of writing according to his own inspiration, rather than along someone else's lines; he was simultaneously rejected in the name of the Wagnerian school, though he professed unlimited admiration for Wagner, in the name of the French school, though he had studied in France and from the French, Bizet in particular, and learned the art of refinements and nuances, and in the name of the Italian school, though he was proud of being and remaining an Italian. Catalani entrusted himself to the judgment of time, and time rendered him justice, but through what and how many vicissitudes!

And this unhappy fellow was the target of immense envy to the point that, on the evening of *Edmea*'s premiere in Milan, some disgraceful people, every restraint overthrown, toasted what they pretended was a fiasco. Atrocious irony! was Catalani's fortune. 'Lucky yes, but only half-lucky,' he'd write himself.[1] On the point of hammering in a nail – his own phrase – the illness of

---

[1] The sentiment appears many times in Catalani's letters to Depanis.

an artist, the distraction of the crowd seduced by a different cry, an unforeseen event would drive him back. Others hammered in the nail. In the meantime, the *lucky* maestro, having knocked in vain at the doors of theatres, waited for two years before placing *Loreley* (and he was already the author of *Elda*, *Dejanice* and *Edmea*) and didn't earn with his art enough to pay for his life so that, sad to say, more than once, lacking the money to accompany them, he allowed his offspring to travel alone around the treacherous world of the theatres.

Catalani had neither failures nor triumphs, what he experienced was worse: he was tolerated. If they kill the weak, failures excite the strong to great works, whether they are accepted with the olympian disdain of a Rossini or reacted to with the vehement impetuosity of a Wagner. Yet it's nice to hear roaring all around the rumble of battle, to throw oneself headlong into the fray, to grapple with the public hand-to-hand, taming it with the strength of genius, compelling it to make amends, forcefully imposing on it the act of homage. To live, to live, it is the struggle that is life; to vegetate while being pitied is death. Such was Catalani's luck.

Catalani obtained the post of Professor of Composition at the Milan Conservatory of Music, which secured him his daily bread, but for him this victory was a source of bitterness. Unable to question his genius and his learning, those in charge of the appointment held his weak health against him, and he remained long suspended between a yes and a no, plagued by the prospect that not being eventually offered the position would signify a sentence close to death. 'I'd regret it much more if I didn't get the post for being a first rate consumptive than for proven inability,' he'd complain; 'I could still prove that I'm not an ass.'[1] He did not mention, alas, the other possibility. Nominated, he honoured the position with scrupulous diligence. Concerned

---

1 Letter of 31 March 1888. Letters 50.

for the future of his students, he applied his broad conception of art to his teaching and carefully tried not to mould them all in the same cast; on the contrary, he'd urge each to follow his own tendency. 'If that particular pupil feels like that, why derail him?' he'd repeat. 'All genres are good as long as they are heartfelt and well played.'[1]

No, life was not happy for this 'lucky fellow,' the last few years in particular. Certain resounding successes drew the public's attention to others, but justice toward these became injustice toward him, and from injustice he'd suffer fiercely. The letter I'm publishing in facsimile is a document of bitter eloquence, we cannot read it without being moved and without noting the maestro's equanimity, as he never pronounced a single word that was less than correct toward colleagues of his who were more favoured by fortune. Eternal dreamer, he would withdraw more and more from the world and by withdrawing more and more he would become irritable and mournful. 'At the end of the day,' he'd lament, 'having a style of one's own must have some value, yet you run the risk that they either don't listen to you or they pity you. To think that I've been working for twelve years!'[2] At times he'd try to react. 'I live like a patient snail,' he'd say, 'who keeps the horns inside ready to put them out at the first chance, and I hope at that point they've become hard enough to pierce at least a couple of critics.'[3] But he would soon retreat within himself: 'The artistic life neither morally nor materially gives me what it ought to. I have bile in my soul and I grow scared at the idea of my future. What a comedy the world is and how

---

1 Letter of 3 August 1890 (the letter Depanis reproduces in facsimile). Letters 81. See above, p. 96 n.2.

2 No statement corresponding to this appears in Catalani's letters to Depanis, though the sentiments can all be found there. Perhaps this is a memory of Catalani's conversation.

3 Letter of 3 August 1890.

tired I am of it!'[1] Oh! if circumstances allowed the publication of Catalani's letters, what a tragic vision of a very unhappy and thwarted existence![2]

Growing deafness added new suffering to the old sufferings. Catalani's hair grew white, his eye sockets more sunken, his cheeks bonier, his body more bent. He wanted to seem happy, and he'd laugh in a shrill way, similar to a hiccup. Suddenly the smile would die on his face, the temporary redness would disappear from his cheeks, and, conversation interrupted, he would stare into the void before him with lost eyes. In the summer he'd drag his tired body to thermal resorts; those who met him at Masino or at Allevard have not forgotten.[3] He'd ask everybody if they had any cough, if they had difficulties breathing, if they suffered from mouthfuls of blood; he'd rebel against the idea that other people's illnesses would reveal symptoms different from his own, and he'd be delighted if someone was cured, hoping to deceive himself as well as others. At Allevard he became friends with a lady who suffered from the same illness, in a relationship cemented by sympathy and resignation, and it was pitiful to see those two pale, thin figures wandering in the park, pausing every moment, smiling sadly and encouraging each other. Oh! what torment for one who caresses a noble dream of art, believes he's able to realize it, senses in his fantasy a whirl of

---

1 Depanis combines statements from letters of 20 January 1887 and 20 August 1889. Letters 36, 65.

2 As noted in the introduction, Carlo Gatti published Catalani's letters to Depanis in 1946.

3 Bagni del Masino in the Italian alps, a small spa popular in summer, and Allevard-les-bains, a spa town in the French alps. In the course of his endless pursuit of good health Catalani had discovered the former by the summer of 1885, when he wrote to Depanis: 'I've been in Masino for twenty days, and I can't tell you how much good this pure, balsamic air, saturated with the scent of the firs and the pines, has done me.' Letters 20. He spent the summers of 1887 and 1888 at Allevard.

original aspirations, then suddenly intuits that between dream and reality comes death, and is continuously reminded of this death by infallible signs, and fears that this death is about to snatch him any day, any hour, any minute! To have not lost his spirit is a sign of rare energy. Art, idolized despite disenchantment, was his defence against the pain and cruelty of life. On his death bed he was still yearning for an ideal of beauty, and suggested to Toscanini, who was attending him with brotherly love, some retouches to the orchestration of *Loreley*. It is said that dying people may have flashes of the afterlife, and I love to believe that in this supreme moment Alfredo Catalani saw the consoling vision of future vindication and in that vision fell asleep in peace.

Unfortunately I was neither able to pay my last respects to my friend while he was alive, nor accompany his remains to eternal rest. In early August 1893 I had gone to Giomein in Valtournenche to climb the Breithorn. I knew Catalani was poorly, but I was unaware of the seriousness of his illness and supposed it to be one of those small crises he had overcome many times. I wrote, however, asking to be informed if the illness showed signs of worsening as I was to be absent for two, or at most three days. It was 6 August. Towards sunset on the 7th I was on the Théodule pass. Through the cold and transparent air a pinkish light was diffused which seemed to kiss the large cone of the Breithorn while the lower side of the glacier, in shadow, became empurpled. On a rock near the refuge-hut, a squatting girl, elbows on knees and her chin on her hands, was looking about at the amphitheatre of enormous mountains; wherever she turned her eyes, nothing but sky and ice. Little by little, with the arrival of twilight, the shadows invaded the tops and the pink faded, became blue, changing into a milky grey-colour. It was a melancholy spectacle, demanding admiration, and insinuating into the spirit a sweet sadness, a sadness drawn from the immensity. Spontaneously, almost as if it were a telepathic phenomenon, there arose in me a memory of the first scene of the fourth act of *La Wally*, where Wally, from the height of the Murzoll, contemplates the sea of ice. The time and the place made me enjoy redoubled a thousand times the exquisite suggestiveness of the scene. Art and reality were fused together, and I was hardly sure whether it was the landscape that had evoked the music's echo or the music that had been materialized into landscape: for a few minutes they were one. The impression had been so strong and immediate that I promised myself I would write to Catalani as soon as I had returned to Turin, certain to please a friend for whom 'praise was like oil for a lamp.'[1]

In the middle of the night we were awoken by blows struck desperately at the refuge door: a catastrophe had occurred. A certain Seiler from Zermatt, together with a guide from the same place, having become detached from a roped party, had plunged onto the Leone glacier on the Italian side of the Matterhorn.[2] The survivors, an Englishman, Seiler's friend, and the second guide, having wandered like madmen from glacier to glacier the entire day, had at last oriented themselves and come to the Thèodule refuge to tell of the disaster and call for help. 'Tell' is not the right word; worn-out, exhausted, rendered unconscious by tiredness and anguish, they expressed themselves in monosyllables while devouring some food and repeatedly sighing; then, their appetite satisfied (they hadn't eaten anything since

---

[1] On 16 August 1884, Catalani wrote to Depanis: 'your letter was like putting oil in a lamp.' Letters 17.

[2] The *Cresta del Leone* (*Lion Ridge*) is the normal Italian route to the summit of the Matterhorn. The accident was widely reported at the time. Andreas Seiler was just nineteen, and the guide who died, Johann Biener, twenty-four. The Englishman who survived was Oscar Gysi of Manchester. See the *Alpine Journal* 16 (1893), 502. Depanis's account of this Alpine tragedy (not mentioned in his 1893 biography) has the effect of poignantly associating Catalani's death with those of Wally and Hagenbach in *La Wally*.

the morning), they fell asleep. At dawn I quickly descended to Giomein while others went to Zermatt to report the disaster and to ensure that someone would go and recover the bodies; from Giomein I headed via Paquier, where the telegraph had not yet arrived, to Châtillon. Late in the evening I arrived in Turin and here a dispatch which had arrived the previous day informed me of Catalani's death as well as the time and day of the funeral which it would by now be impossible for me to attend.[1] What an agonizing concatenation of events! As I was promising myself to write to him, unaware of what had happened, Catalani had been resting on his death bed for twelve hours, his head emaciated, his beautiful, thoughtful eyes closed, his bony hands placed together. I could neither write to him again, nor see any more my dear, unforgettable friend ...

---

[1] Depanis had arrived back in Turin late on Tuesday evening; the funeral was in Milan at 9 o'clock Wednesday morning.

**Facsimile of Catalani's Letter to Depanis of
3 August 1890**

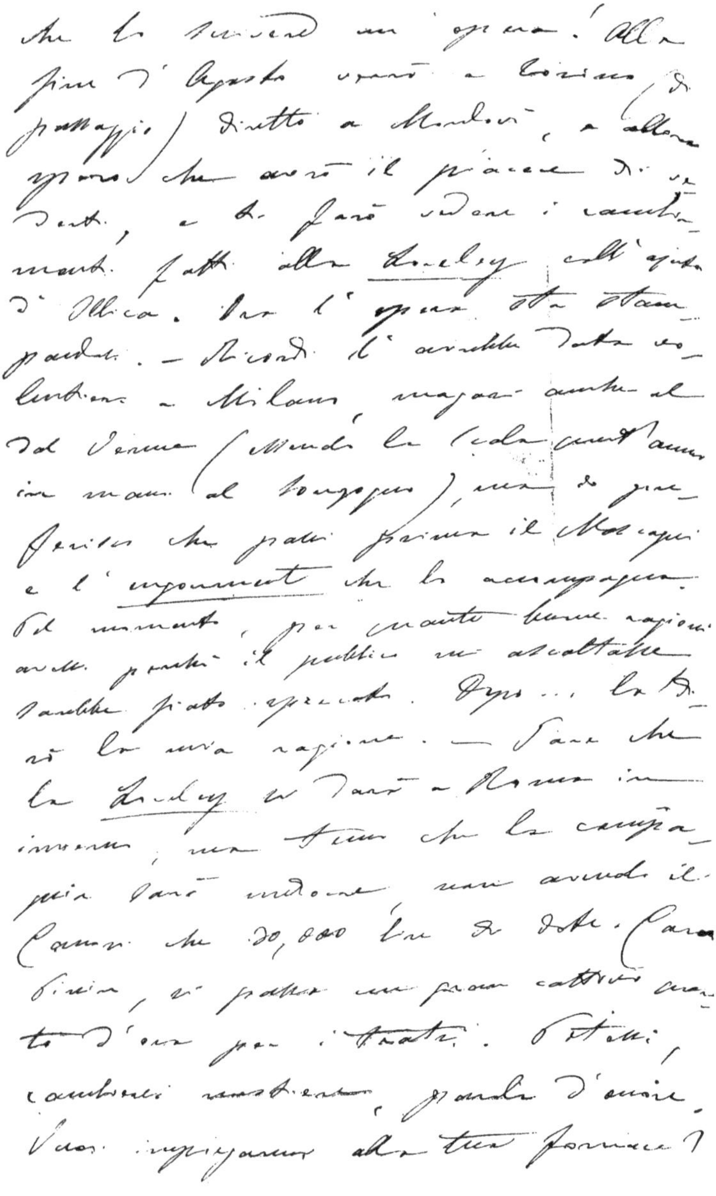

Ti assicuro che farò il mio dovere bene, e non sarò distratto! Sarò un modello d'impiegato — Quest'anno a proposito dei saggi al Conservatorio, mi si è gridata la croce addosso perchè ho lasciato sfoggiare un po' troppo qualche mio allievo nelle cosidette regioni dell'avvenire. Io non ho risposto che una sola cosa: se quel dato mio allievo sente così perchè dovrei deviarlo? tutti i generi in musica son buoni, purchè sentiti e fatti bene... Ma sì... ci vuol altro a contentar tutti. Di nuovo ti prego, impiegami alla tua farmacia, sarò molto meglio. Per lo meno avrò a mia disposizione tanti mattoni... per rompere la testa, anche a chi non me la fa. Addio, amico mio carissimo. Tanti saluti cordiali e affettuosi alla tua cara famiglia. Ricordami al dottor Carlo, e ricevi un abbraccio del tuo

affezionatissimo

Catalani

Stefano Stampa. Self-portrait

Letters to Stefano Stampa, 1875–1885

Alfredo Catalani

[Originally published in Ezio Flori, *Il Figliastro del Manzoni, Stefano Stampa* (1939), vol. 2, pp. 127–31, 151–52, 193–94, 285–86.][1]

*R*EGARDING ALFREDO *Catalani, we find that in spring 1875 he already had a solid friendship with Stefano Stampa. In 1873 the young musician from Lucca had moved from the Paris Conservatoire to the Milan Conservatory, and at this time he was putting the finishing touches to* La Falce, *with libretto by Arrigo Boito (*Tobia Gorio*). This was performed in the small theatre of the Conservatory on 17 July [1875].*[2] *The short work, for soloists, chorus, and orchestra caused a sensation, and not just among interested critics; the public immediately understood that here was an exceptional musical temperament. The Società del Quartetto, of which Stefano was a member, accepted the prologue of* La Falce *for performance as part of their concert series. Surely Stefano knew Catalani's little opera, and surely he undertook to have the society accept the prologue. But we know nothing about their*

---

1 The letters are given here complete with Flori's commentary. Paragraphing in the letters is conjectural: Flori published them in a continuous block of text.

2 Actually 19 July.

first meeting, or what led to the reciprocal friendship between the young composer and Manzoni's son-in-law. Let us repeat, however, that their friendship was already solid in spring *1875*. In an undated letter that must have been written in March or April *1875*[1] – Stefano was already in Torricella by then – Catalani is very anxious that his friend be able to attend the performance of La Falce.

Dear Count,

If I did not reply immediately to your dear letter, it was because I would not have been able to tell you anything precise about the performance of my little opera either yesterday or the day before. Even today I can't be specific about the day it will be performed. From what the director told me this morning, however, I understand that it will be between the 15th and the 20th of June, and not at the end of May, as I was hoping and desiring. The principal cause of this delay is the difficulty of my ugly music, which needs to be rehearsed a long time so that it makes the least pitiful impression possible. Will you be able to be in Milan at that time? I would be very unhappy if this delay were to cause me to be deprived of your judgment, which I desire no matter how fierce it may be. If it is really fierce, I will be able to form valid criteria for myself by which to judge my music's worth. Dispassionate and consequently true judgments are so rare that those one receives are valued very dearly. I hope that I will receive such judgments from you.

[*Given Catalani's artistic tendencies, his judgment on Wagner is very balanced. The letter continues:*[2]]

---

[1] In fact the letter cannot have been written earlier than around 10 May. See note 1 on next page.

[2] This is Flori's comment.

The success of *Lohengrin* in London, denied in *Il Pungolo* though confirmed in *La Perseveranza*, is a new victory won by our musical camp.[1] I take delight in it with all my heart. Wagner's genre as he conceives of it is certainly not the sort that will prevail in the future, but the latter will, without any doubt, resemble what he does. For that reason we need to rejoice every time we hear that the music of the great German has triumphed.

Nothing new in Milan. It's extraordinarily hot here, which very much makes me want to finish my *burdens* quickly so that I can go and breathe a little mountain air. I think that I will spend several days in Switzerland or Santa Caterina nella Valtellina in July. I will be very happy if I can see you in Milan on the 28th. I will hasten to come and get you.

With a thousand friendly and respectful best wishes, please believe me to be your most devoted and indebted servant,

Alfredo Catalani.[2]

We can be sure that Stefano must have initiated a discussion about music while Catalani was worrying about La Falce. *The latter wrote to Stampa on 19 June:*

---

1 *Lohengrin*, sung in Italian, was brought out at Covent Garden on 8 May 1875. This was only the second production of a Wagner opera in Britain. In 1870 Drury Lane had presented *Der Fliegende Holländer* (in Italian, as *L'Olandese Dannato*), but it had made little impact. Between 1870 and 1875 the British public had become far more aware of Wagner, however, so *Lohengrin* prompted great curiosity and was surprisingly successful. Hermann Klein later recalled that 'the opera was received with a warmth that grew and grew till it culminated in a tremendous climax of enthusiasm. The "tooth-and-nail" opponents of Wagner, who flourished exceedingly in London at this time, were simply dumbfounded' (see *Thirty Years of Musical Life in London, 1870–1900* [London, 1903], 44).

2 Such flowery epistolary closings were common in nineteenth-century Italian letters, especially when written to the nobility. They are omitted from the subsequent letters.

I received your very dear letters, which I would like to answer at length today. But unfortunately it's already late. I therefore have to put that off until another day, which, however, will be very soon. Meanwhile I send you these few lines to tell you that nothing has been decided definitely as to when my little opera will be performed. They say that it will be at the end of the month. That is, however, a 'they say' that I hope and desire will come to pass. Because I am very tired of waiting. This delay results from a desire to wait until two other short operas by two of my colleagues are ready. I am impatient to see my work performed because I am afraid that you will no longer be able to come to Milan after June, because it seems that you told me that in July you had to be absent from Lombardy. I really want you to hear and judge my music, because your judgment seems very true to me. Please excuse me, dear Count.

Alfredo Catalani

Catalani's anxiety increased in the first days of July. He wrote to Stefano on 2 July:

Dear Count,

You cannot believe how many problems I have had in the last few days, always because of my ever so famous *little opera*. Even my health has been affected by it a little. Today, however, I am well. I hope that you will be willing to forgive me if I didn't keep the promise that I made to write you a long letter. I didn't forget about it, though, no, certainly not. Indeed, I thought about writing you every day, but my ideas were *bouleversées* [disordered, Fr.], and as a result I wasn't ever able to do it. It seems that everything has finally been decided and cleared up, and that the performance of my opera will take place Saturday at 8:00. Friday, as a result, the dress rehearsal will take place. It would not, however, come as a surprise if these two dates, announced today, were to be changed tomorrow. For that reason I will write to you again in two or three days. Then I will be able to let you know the date decided on with greater certainty. I repeat that the thought of having you present at my first *debut* gives me immense pleasure. It is just that I would not want you to go to any great inconvenience on account of me. Indeed, coming here to Milan in this heat certainly won't be very pleasant. I therefore beg you not to be kind to me just for kindness' sake; if that were the case, I would be very sad.

Alfredo Catalani

Stefano continued the discussion of matters musical, and in particular – presumably – those concerning the opposition between Verdi and Wagner. Regarding Verdi, Catalani came out with a judgment that we shall limit ourselves to calling very strange (6 July).

Dear Count,

I received your very dear letter, which I found full of very correct ideas. You ask me how I would explain Verdi's *European* success. It's true that it's rather difficult to answer. It is a fact that his success exists. But I firmly maintain that it is not the result of the merit of his music, which is not that great. I also believe that politics must have had a large part in this success, especially in Vienna. Blessed politics! They get in everywhere and hurt everything, nothing more so than the arts. In spite of all the reasons that can be cited to explain his success, however, it's a fact that it is an indication of decadence. Let's hope for a future reawakening (*risorgimento*); it can't fail to take place, certainly, since the world moves forward like a wheel. As a result, good must follow bad and vice versa. I compare Verdi to the poets of the sixteenth century, who made the public delirious with their hyperbole. Verdi makes them delirious with screams and stage effects void of common sense instead. Forgive my spiel. If it seems to you that I've said too many bad things about the great colossus of contemporary music, I want you to correct me in my judgments if that is possible.

The performance of my little opera is still scheduled for Saturday evening. There will certainly be a performance that evening. I don't know, however, if it will be in the form of a dress rehearsal or the first performance. That will depend on the theatre director. I therefore hope to be able to see you very soon. I will have the tickets and the opera's libretto left for you at the entrance of your lodgings, as you ask.

Alfredo Catalani

La Falce was put off again. Catalani wrote from Milan to Stampa again on 7 July:

Dear Count,

For various reasons the performance of my little opera has been put off to Wednesday evening. As a result, the dress rehearsal will take place Monday. I wrote you a letter yesterday that I hope you received.

Alfredo Catalani

And it was put off again – and, fortunately, for the last time – to the next Saturday, 17 July. We can be sure, though nothing in the letters says so, that Stefano attended that first performance. Afterwards Catalani travelled to the lake region near Milan, promising himself that he would spend a week in Venice before returning to Lucca. But it seems that he already had his next opera, Elda, *in mind, as appears in this letter to Stefano dated 10 August 1875 from Milan:*

Dear Count,

Please allow me to send you these few lines in place of a postcard. I returned to Milan yesterday. I found your two postcards here, and now today I received another one. I thank you from the bottom of my heart for the interest that you're taking in me. I would, however, like to be more deserving of it. I took a little trip to Lake Maggiore and Lake Como and derived great benefit from it. In just a few days I have changed my way of seeing everything. Now, however, I will have to bear yet further burdens, since I have to conduct my little opera for another two or three performances. It will be repeated Saturday evening along with the other two. There will be a lot of antagonism as a result. I'll remain in Milan until the 25th of this month. Then I will leave for Venice, where I will remain for a week. Then I will return to my birthplace.

No matter where I am, I will never forget either you or your dear friendship, and I promise to send you news of me often ... on the condition, however, that I also want to have news of you. This winter we will talk about music, and as I compose some new pieces for the opera that I have to write, I will have You listen to them and You will give me your judgment, which is always so fair and thought through.

Alfredo Catalani

The success enjoyed by the prologue to La Falce *when performed by the Società del Quartetto confirmed the worth of the opera and Catalani's magnificent musical temperament. It created a warm atmosphere of sympathy for him. The craving for an immediate, larger, and definitive success promptly set him back to work. In Lucca in September Catalani produced the voice and piano reduction of* La Falce, *which was then published by Casa Lucca, and looked for a subject for a libretto for his next opera, about which he wanted to consult Stampa. On Friday 4 September [1875] he wrote from Lucca:*

Dear Count,

I've been here with my family for three days. I left Milan later than I expected. I have to return there soon to deal with Casa Lucca concerning the choice of a *libretto* for the new opera that I have to write. Meanwhile, I'm working on the piano arrangement of my *Falce*. It very much displeased me not to be able to see you the last time you came to Milan. I would have liked to ask you for advice regarding the choice of subject for the libretto. I hope, however, to be able to see you at the end of the month, since in your last letter you told me that you intend to see the Fine Arts Exhibition. I will be in Milan around the 22nd. I'll stay there a week, I think, and then go to Bologna to hear Boito's *Mefistofele*. Will you come? I'm very curious to hear that opera. My health is very good. I would very much like to have news of you. I therefore request that you favour me with a line.

Alfredo Catalani

Boito's Mefistofele, *which had failed noisily at La Scala in March 1868, was being readied for a revival at Bologna's Teatro Comunale in October 1875. The Bolognese public's judgment must have very much interested the young maestro from Lucca, who had similar if not identical musical tendencies to those of Boito.*[1] *He arrived in Milan on the last day of September, and on 2 October wrote to Stampa:*

Dear Count,

I arrived here the other evening. Various circumstances delayed my arrival. I passed by your lodgings and learned with displeasure that you were not in Milan. I'm afraid that we won't be able to see each other until November. I'll be here a few days; then I will go to Bologna to hear Boito's *Mefistofele*. And in the first days of next month I will return here to set to work on writing my opera.

---

1 The *Mefistofele* produced in 1875 was in fact a heavily revised version of the opera that had failed in 1868. Jay Nicolaisen summarises: 'The work that emerged in 1875 was a popularized version of the first *Mefistofele*. ... Boito planned his revisions with two goals in mind: (1) discarding everything that had offended the ears of the La Scala audience of 1868; and (2) bolstering what remained by the addition of pieces that were certain to please.' In its revised form *Mefistofele* proved a great success. Catalani probably already knew Boito (the librettist of *La Falce*) quite well, and had doubtless been privy to some of the artistic issues surrounding *Mefistofele*.

I think I've found a subject. It will be *Loreley*. There's a little of the fantastic in it, which won't be bad for me, since I very much like that genre. I don't know if I should be happy or sad about that tendency, though! My health is very good.

Alfredo Catalani

Please forgive me for writing to you in such haste.

It was not yet Loreley; *but the same legend, transferred by Carlo d'Ormeville, the librettist, to the shores of the Baltic, was adapted to make the libretto for* Elda.

* * *

Alfredo Catalani had been struck by the first symptoms of that slow but inexorable illness that, fifteen years later, would cut short his splendid activity in its most beautiful flowering. He had virtually fled to Lucca, where the attentions of his family and the native air had given him strength again. He wrote to his friend Stampa, giving him personal news and asking for the same with that lively affection that enlarged their friendship to something like a family relationship. This time he was mistaken with regard to the first three parts of the Wagnerian tetralogy ... .[1] *He wrote to Stampa on 13 August 1878 from Massa Pisana, near Lucca:*

Dear Count,

You will be astonished to receive a letter from me. I am writing to you first of all to ask for news of you, which I want to know. Secondly, to tell you the reason that has kept me from writing to you until now, although I wanted to do so for some time. I have been sick for more than two months. Now I'm convalescing, but

---

[1] Catalani was in fact being quite correct: Wagner himself described *Der Ring des Nibelungen* as a trilogy with a *Vorabend* (preliminary evening). Giuseppe Depanis consistently refers to the work as a trilogy in his various critical writings on Wagner.

my health is not yet perfect. I started to feel ill around the end of June. I was forced to stay in bed and remained there all through July with a very high fever caused by my digestive system. I started to feel alright in the first days of August, and got out of bed and ate with an appetite. I even left the house. Every day I got stronger, until one evening the fever came back in a violent fashion. Not wanting to get sick again in Milan, I came to Lucca right away. As soon as I got here I went back to bed and stayed there another twelve long days. Now I am fairly well. I'm in the country with my family in a house in the hills outside Lucca, and here I hope to recover completely. Then around the middle of October I will return to the Lombard capital.[1]

And you, dear Count, how are you? If you have a few free moments, I beg you to give me news of you. Will we resume our artistic discussions this winter? Sometimes we have fairly divergent opinions, but I believe that we will end up agreeing completely. Have you worked any more on your *Requiem*? I would like to see it finished. I believe that the complete Wagnerian Trilogy will be performed in Munich in the month of August.[2] Did you read anything about that in *La Perseveranza*? I would have liked to have heard it. (I bet that, instead of saying *hear it*, you would have said *see it*!) I believe it will be difficult for that music to cross the Alps. As a result, sooner or later we will have to cross them to hear it. By 'that music' I mean only the Trilogy, not Wagner's other operas, a fair number of which have already arrived here in Italy. If you have the goodness to write to me, you can send the letter to Lucca, via San Nicolao. From there they bring letters up here to us in the hills every day.

Alfredo Catalani

Father and Mother send you their best wishes.

---

1 I.e. Milan.

2 In fact, after various delays, the *Ring* was finally performed at Munich between 17 and 23 November – the first complete cycle outside Bayreuth.

Catalani did, in fact, return 'to the Lombard capital' in autumn, having to go to Turin for the audition of his Elda, *which had been introduced by Ippolito Valletta*[1] *and very strongly championed by the music publisher, Giovannina Lucca, Catalani's patron.*

* * *

Stefano had also shaken Alfredo Catalani from his torpor. Parsifal *was given at Bayreuth at the end of July. The year before, Boito's* Mefistofele, *staged by the composer, had triumphed at La Scala. Catalani had finished* Dejanice, *to a libretto by Zanardini, and was starting to worry. On the 24th of what we presume to be September*[2] *in what was certainly 1882 (neither month nor year is indicated on the letter) he wrote to Stampa from Milan:*

I have thought about writing to you several times, and I would have done so if I had known where to write to you. But I never managed to find the piece of paper on which you wrote your address the last time you were at my house. Therefore your letter today, which like all the others is very dear to me, also reaches me at a very opportune moment, since it allows me, finally, to be able to fulfil a wish of mine, and a promise.

I didn't go to Lake Como. Instead, I spent some twenty days at Lake Maggiore, which, to tell the truth, I like much more. The brief sojourn there at the lake did me a lot of good as during that time I tried not to work, to the extent that that was possible for me. And I will say that I succeeded completely, and even easily. I will leave Milan in a few days for Tuscany, where my family is anxiously awaiting me.

---

1 For Valletta, a close friend of Catalani's, see above, p. 45 n. 3.

2 It seems almost certain to have been August, given what Catalani says about the possibility of going to Bayreuth to see *Parsifal,* which had its last performance on 29 August. By 22 September Catalani would have been well aware that he had missed the opportunity to see the production.

I have set aside, necessarily, the thought of going to Bayreuth. I looked high and low for a ticket. For a moment I thought I had found one ... it seemed to me that I was already listening to that most original and (sometimes) sublime music! But the illusion vanished quickly. Some very intelligent individuals assure me that this work of Wagner's is much less asphyxiating than *Tristan and Isolde*. (I said *asphyxiating*, but in the best sense of the word. Even the best perfume in this world can asphyxiate if used to excess. I don't know if I have expressed my thoughts well.)

They're talking, or rather thinking about giving my opera next winter at La Scala. If this idea were to become reality, would it be good or bad for me? Who knows! Did you also see *Mefistofele*? I ask your permission, dear Count, to take the score of *Guglielmo Tell*[1] with me to Lucca. Is it true that you'll allow me to do so?

Alfredo Catalani

Dejanice *was in fact given at La Scala on 17 March 1883, with success, although Depanis judged it to be 'an unhappy reheating of material from* L'Africana, Aida *and* La Gioconda *served up in a Greek sauce.'*[2]

* * *

Catalani, who had come to Milan – presumably for his Edmea *– wrote to Stampa on 29 August [1885].*[3]

---

1 Rossini's opera (1829).

2 See above, pp. 77–78.

3 The date makes no sense, given what Catalani says at the end of the letter about having delivered his opera, which can be assumed to be *Edmea*. In August he had barely started work on it, and was not in Milan: Letters 20-21. The letter must have been written rather later in the year, perhaps on 29 November, and presumably before 17 December when Catalani wrote to Antonio Ghislanzoni, his librettist, '*Edmea* will go on [at La Scala] at the end of January.' Letters 21.

Dear Count,

I came here two days ago. I came to see if it is possible to arrange something for my opera. For the moment I don't know anything, or rather no one knows anything, because things are dark, as they were a month ago, at both the Bologna theatre and La Scala.

I received your two very interesting letters about Wagner and his music. Let's *fight* a little this winter about that. Are you willing? I stopped by your house today. I thought I might find you there, because I know that you come to Milan every year when the Fine Arts Exhibition is open. If you haven't been to it already, and if you are coming in the next few days, I would be very happy to be able to meet you. I will stay in Milan until Tuesday or Wednesday of next week, if nothing happens that keeps me from leaving. I will return to Tuscany. I'm no longer at 9 corso di Porta Nuova, but instead at 10 via Milazzo. I tried to go to Varese as conductor of the theatre orchestra, but today I learned that they have already hired a conductor. I would have liked to spend a season there, now that I have nothing to do, having delivered my opera a month and a half ago. Forgive me, dear Count, for my long silence.

Alfredo Catalani

Edmea *was performed at La Scala in March 1886.*[1]

---

1 In fact the premiere was on 27 February.

Hina Spani (1896–1969),
who recorded arguably the finest version of
'Ebben ne andro lontana.'

Catalani on Record: The 78 Era

Stanley Henig

RECORDED SOUND has been part of our lives for around 110 years. For half this period, the normal medium was the shellac record playing at approximately seventy eight revolutions per minute. As a medium its suitability for longer works was always in question: a complete opera performance might run to thirty or more sides. However, it was ideal for the operatic aria. There are certainly no complete versions of Catalani's operas on 78rpm, but there are numerous recordings of arias from his operas as well as the odd duet. Discounting repeat versions – sometimes for different companies – by the same singer, I have identified around 115 separate recordings. I have, perhaps arbitrarily, included versions by three singers whose recording careers overlapped the 78rpm and long playing eras: Mario del Monaco, Magda Olivero and Renata Tebaldi. In all those recordings feature around 80 artists, many of whom appeared in staged performances of Catalani's operas. With the help of friends and fellow collectors I have been able to listen to rather more than half the recordings and in this short essay will discuss a selection, particularly concentrating on the better versions and the more important artists.

It is perhaps no surprise that almost all the recorded items are from *Loreley* and *La Wally*: two arias from *Dejanice* are the exception. There are more records from *La Wally* than from *Loreley*, but this is mainly on account of the disproportionately large number of sopranos performing 'Ebben ne andro lontana.' The aria was brought to a wider audience by the film *Diva*, but it has been a showpiece for sopranos for very much longer. There are extant versions on 78 by more than 45 singers, accounting for almost half the total number of records. This being the case, and given that some of the sopranos in question also recorded other items from Catalani operas, the aria offers a good starting point for a comparative review.

La Wally

In many ways 'Ebben' is a cruel piece: it requires range, ability and power. I think it should ideally start rather wistfully. The heroine, described as a child of nature, might well seem a less strange character today, but underlying the aria is the fact that she is more or less being forced to leave home. The aria ends climactically on a theme of 'no turning back.' Three of the greatest and earliest sopranos who made recordings essayed the aria. Teresa Arkel (1861–1929) was probably past her best. She starts contemplatively but once the music becomes more dramatic the voice spreads alarmingly under pressure. Salomea Kruszelnicka (1873–1952) was a great dramatic soprano but I find little characterization in her interpretation and her voice, too, spreads towards the end. Ester Mazzoleni (1883–1982) gives a much softer opening and at times her version is quite moving, but then, like the other two, she comes under pressure towards the end. It is interesting to note that whilst almost all interpreters of Wally are from the Italian school of singing, Arkel and Kruszelnicka originated from Polish Galicia. Much less well known is Ebe Boccolini (1889–?). Hers is not the most memorable account, but she handles the piece with relative ease. It is worth bearing in mind that until the mid 1920s all records were made by the acoustic method with the performers literally singing or playing into a horn. The arrival of the electrical method would mean a huge improvement in recording quality.

Moving on in time we encounter Maria Farneti (1877–1955). She was the first to sing Wally in Buenos Aires as early as 1904 and first recorded the aria for the Fonotipia company in 1917. This was still in the era of acoustic recording, but the sound is very much more modern than those already discussed. Farneti's first version is a demonstration by a great dramatic soprano at her best: powerful and moving without any hint of strain at the climax. There could not be a greater contrast than the interpretation by Juanita Carraciolo (1888–1924). Perhaps on account of her short life, almost entirely devoted to singing, she seems to have been virtually forgotten until the recent publication of a biography by Roberta Paganelli. I suspect she probably sang Wally more often than any other performer, except for Ersilde Cervi Caroli (1884–1964) whose small recorded legacy does not include 'Ebben.' Happily Carraciolo did record it almost at the end of her life and career and with some ninety stage performances of the role behind her. In contrast to the dramatic emotion of Farneti, Carraciolo is much more reflective and contemplative: a lovely piece of singing! The very last of these early singers is Giuseppina Baldassare-Tedeschi (1881–1961). It seems to me a remarkable voice; her interpretation is mid-way between those of Farneti and Carraciolo and she handles all aspects of the music with ease and skill. However, there is a postscript to this discussion of acoustic recordings. As late as 1931 Farneti re-recorded the aria, this time for Italian Columbia, and there is a significant change in her interpretation. Farneti in 1931 is more contemplative, even sorrowful. She sounds completely inside the role: no longer a dramatic soprano but Wally. One of the truly great records!

Farneti is joined at the pinnacle by two other great sopranos whose careers covered both the acoustic and electric eras. Claudia Muzio (1889–1936) is best known for a series of late recordings for Columbia. Earlier she had made recordings for Pathé and Edison and both series included 'Ebben.' Both companies made vertical rather than laterally cut records and there are some complications with domestic reproduction. I much prefer the 1920 Edison – one of the truly great versions. It is well recorded and Muzio is totally inside the role: the result is far more wistful and reflective than the Pathé record. The short repeated phrase 'mai piu' is incredibly moving – never again will Wally return! Muzio was a great singer, and this version might have pride of place but for the 1928 rendering by Hina Spani (1896–1969). Born in Argentina, she enjoyed a hugely successful career throughout Italy and across South America. Practically all her records were made by the electrical process. Essentially a lyrical spinto soprano she uses her voice with the greatest sensitivity. There are no problems with the dramatic conclusion of the aria and hers is surely the finest version ever recorded.

So as not to overload this essay with consideration of all the numerous recordings of Catalani's best known aria, I want to make just brief mention of a few of the many other versions. Maria Luisa Fanelli (1900–88) is another who is scarcely remembered today. Born into an Italian family in Chicago, she had a shortish career which seems to have been exclusively in Italy. Her 1930 'Ebben' reveals a beautiful voice – lyrical and caressing. Like many others she is, though, sorely pressed by the climactic conclusion to the piece. Iva Pacetti (1898–1981) enjoyed a considerable career in Italy, especially at La Scala, Milan. She also sang extensively in South America. As with most of her recordings, her 'Ebben' is a good performance although I do not find it that memorable. Carla Castellani (1906–2005) debuted and sang extensively at La Scala from 1941; she made a very few records for HMV in 1946, but little seems to be known of her thereafter. Hers is a warm and attractive voice – in timbre it sounds more like a mezzo soprano, but she has no difficulty with any part of the aria. I very much like this version and think it well worth seeking out! Another version from late in the 78 era is by Joan Hammond (1912–96), seemingly the only English speaking singer to record the aria. She often performed and recorded in English translations. Not on this occasion: indeed, I do not know of any recording in other than Italian – perhaps no translated singing versions are available.

Finally, we come to Renata Tebaldi (1922–2004) and Magda Olivero (1910–). Tebaldi's 1950 Cetra record was recorded a few years before she first sang the role on stage in December 1953 at La Scala. Like so many of Tebaldi's subsequent recordings, the singing is beautiful, and she manages all the difficulties of the aria, including the ending, with consummate ease. But I find her slightly lacking in characterization and so, in the last analysis, the interpretation does not linger in the memory. Of course Tebaldi continued to sing the role on stage and there are various complete recordings available. Amongst relatively modern singers she is the Wally of reference, but I cannot help wondering if this really ought to be the case. Olivero is somehow timeless. She made her operatic debut in 1933, her first commercial recordings five years later, and was still active during the 1980s. Truly she was one of the very greatest singers of the last century. The bulk of her recordings are live rather than studio based and exact dates are not always certain. Her version of 'Ebben' has all the right lights and shades. Truly this is a great interpretation to go alongside those of Farneti, Muzio and Spani.

Wally's decision to leave her home at the end of the first act is occasioned by her father's demand that she marry Gellner, whom she does not love. There is a strange early acoustic recording of the passage which precedes 'Ebben' by Domenico Viglione-Borghese (1877–1957) and Giannina Russ (1873–1951). Strange in context and perhaps not really a duet. Wally is merely conversational whilst Gellner sings a potentially and, given his character, almost strangely beautiful aria, 'T'amo ben io' – sentiments which hardly needs translating. The baritone aria was also recorded by Riccardo Stracciari (1875–1955), Renato Zanelli (1892–1935) and Gino Bechi (1913–93), and there is a considerable contrast in the performances. The Chilean Zanelli achieved greatest fame as a tenor, singing Tristan and Otello, but he began as a baritone. His 1919 version of 'T'amo ben io' is surely one of the most beautiful pieces of singing on record: totally belying Gellner's character as it emerges in Act Three. Viglione-Borghese certainly attempts to make it a paean to love although in a slightly rough voice. Bechi is perhaps too matter of fact, but Stracciari, normally one of the great baritones, seems to me to have no real feel for the aria at all.

The beginning of Act Three finds a sad and almost despondent Wally: 'Né mai dunque avrò pace?' – when shall I know peace again. My personal favourite version is the 1924 recording by Carmen Melis (1885–1967). Her powerful dramatic voice would have surely made her an ideal interpreter of Wally, but I find no evidence that she ever sang the role on stage. She was, incidentally, the leading Italian interpreter of the fearsome role of Minnie in Puccini's *La Fanciulla del West* and probably sang it more often than anybody else in operatic history. Seemingly all her records were made by the acoustic method and the version of 'Né mai dunque' was the very last she made in 1924. It is a wonderful piece of singing – tragic and powerful at the beginning, softening with nostalgic recollections of youth, and dramatically sustained at the end. Gina Cigna (1900–2001) made her recording under far more favourable conditions: the fine orchestral accompaniment demonstrates the advantages of electrical recording. Hers was a powerful dramatic soprano with a cutting edge. I am not sure she softens sufficiently at 'La giovinezza,' but given the quality of the recording and the accompaniment this remains a disc of reference.

Another version worthy of consideration is that of Giannina Russ. In 1909 she actually recorded two pieces with Viglione-Borghese: I think it is a misuse of the term to describe either as 'duets.' Gellner re-appears in act three – still claiming to be passionately in love with Wally but now revealing himself as a thoroughly nasty character. He sings of his hatred for Hagenbach, the beloved of Wally, and this piece is recorded together with the first part of 'Né mai dunque.' Viglione-Borghese's voice is much more appropriate on this occasion, whilst it is difficult to judge Russ. However the Fonotipia company which recorded these two 'duets' were nothing if not consistent in their championship of Catalani, and Russ recorded the full aria the following year. It opens slightly discursively and I find the tempo a little on the fast side. The sadness comes through and the voice softens when Wally thinks back to youth's ardent dreams – the part omitted in the earlier version.

Whether attributable to quirkiness or cost saving, there is another strange Fonotipia recording from the beginning of the final act. Wally's real friend is Walter, a zither player, and they have a fond farewell dominated by Wally's aria 'Prendi, fanciul, e serbala!' The only version I know is that of Maria Farneti. The few lines for Walter, a 'trouser role,' are also sung by Farneti without any evident vocal transformation. The aria itself is deeply moving – one of the finest of the Catalani records. It is with a piece towards the end of the opera that the tenor makes his sole appearances on any of these 78s. There are a very few records of 'M'hai salvato' and I have only managed to hear the version by Pablo Civil (1899–1987). He enjoyed an international career, particularly in Italy. Like other Spanish tenors his is an open-throated style of singing well suited to the character of Hagenbach. Wally's few lines are sung by Maria Vinciguerra.

Dejanice

Having covered the major 78rpm recordings from *La Wally*, and before considering the legacy of discs from *Loreley*, I will have a brief look at *Dejanice*. I have heard three versions of Admeto's romance 'Mia bianca amor' and one of the bass aria 'O patria mia' – and these are very likely the sum total. Nino Piccaluga (1890–1973) sang extensively in Europe and North America. His is a big, strong voice and the style almost declamatory. The words give the obvious context for the romance, but this performance is hardly very caressing. Salvatore Pollicino (1888–1961) appeared on stage in both *La Wally* and *Loreley*. He too is rather declamatory in style and I detect a slightly whiney element in the timbre. In fact my preferred version is by the more recent artist Salvatore Puma (1920–). He enjoyed a wide international career. There is more light and shade in his performance, and the words are caressed rather than declaimed. The interpreter of the bass aria is Luciano Neroni (1909–51). Early death shortly before a scheduled debut at the Metropolitan in New York surely prevented a major international career and Neroni taking his true place in the line of Italian bass singers, perhaps in direct succession to Tancredi Pasero. In his memorable 1948 recording Neroni's rolling bass offers fine shading as well as a deep and powerful voice.

Loreley

Like *La Wally*, this opera too revolves around the eponymous heroine – a character drawn from Germanic myth and legend. The bulk of the extracts on 78 feature Loreley herself and the recorded legacy includes performances by many fine singers. In contrast with *La Wally*, there is a showpiece aria for tenor, 'Nel verde maggio.' It is a lovely piece which hardly heralds the horrors to come. The great Beniamino Gigli (1890–1957) offers a characteristic honeyed performance. For sheer beauty of singing Gigli has few if any rivals. The acoustic recording made in New York early in 1923 is wonderfully lyrical. Other recorded versions to note are by Amadeo Berdini (1920–64), Mario del Monaco (1915–82), Giuseppe Garutti (1895–?) and Vittorio Rè (1891–1984). Unsurprisingly they all lack the wonderful lyricism of Gigli, but a rather harder sound may express the character of Walter more appropriately. Del Monaco's late 78 came relatively early in his career, but the tendency to over-loudness was already evident: I do not detect a great deal of feeling in his version and find Berdini and Rè rather more cultured. In fact the former was developing what should have been an important international career covering bel-canto, *verismo* and much more modern operas prior to his early death. As far as is known Rè's career was almost exclusively in Italy, mostly in *verismo* roles. He made six records for Fonotipia in 1921.

The relaxed atmosphere of a river walk remains for Loreley's first aria 'Da che tutta,' preceded by an exchange with an unknown tenor in the recording by Kruszelnicka. Her rich, warm voice seems much more at home here than in the big aria from *La Wally* discussed above. But the atmosphere starts to change with 'Non fiu da un padre,' when Loreley sings about her life to date. Three singers represent the oldest school of recording artists: Ester Mazzoleni, already encountered in this essay with her version of 'Ebben,' Eugenia Burzio (1872–1922) and Celestina Boninsegna (1877–1947). All are worthy of consideration. Mazzoleni seems to me more successful here than with the aria from *La Wally*, although at times her voice does sound under pressure. Burzio, who recorded the aria in 1905, starts quietly with sorrow about her upbringing very much in evidence. She does not overplay the drama and this could be a reason for some finding this version preferable to that of the 1917 rendering by Boninsegna, whose performance is perhaps exactly what we would expect from one of the greatest dramatic sopranos on record. She richly conveys both the tragedy and sorrow. Boninsegna's record incorporates the preceding lines of Loreley's duet with Walter, but Luigi Bolis does not have enough to sing to make much impression. There is a very much fuller version of the whole scena recorded electrically for Fonotipia by Etty Maroli and Giuseppe Garutti. Apart from the fact that both were active in the 1920s and 1930s I have been unable to find much about their lives and careers. Even in the extended version Garutti has little chance to make much of an impact. The timbre of Maroli's voice suggests a mezzo. If at times her style of singing suggests she is almost swallowing her words, she is nonetheless a very credible Loreley, even if nothing like as fine a singer as Boninsegna. Finally it is worth mentioning Winifred Cecil (1907–85) if only as one of the very small band of English speaking artists who recorded arias by Catalani. Hers was a relatively late recording for Cetra: well etched but in the last analysis it makes much less impact than earlier versions.

At the very end of Act One there are two linked passages/arias for Loreley – 'Dove sono....O forze recondite.' Broken hearted she calls on Alberich, who is to transform her from her human self to the mythical water maiden or siren. This time I have nothing but praise for Ester Mazzoleni, who superbly charts the evolution from sorrow and tragedy to anger – a reminder that in her relatively short career she was indeed a soprano assoluta. She did, incidentally, appear quite often in both *Dejanice* and *Loreley* and probably sang 'Ebben' in concert. Claudia Muzio follows Mazzoleni in singing 'Dove sono' but only part of what follows: it is lovely singing, but the dramatic impulse of the entire 'O forze' would surely have over-stretched her vocal resources. Not so for the dramatic soprano Bianca Scacciati (1894–1948). She enjoyed a major career at La Scala singing some of the great dramatic roles in the Italian repertoire, whilst at the Costanzi in Rome she was the first to sing Turandot. Scacciati goes straight into a full version of 'O forze' and this 1929 record is simply a 'tour de force'! Vocal agility and pyrotechnics come together in what must be one of the most remarkable pieces of soprano singing on record and she makes it sound easy!

At the beginning of the second act we are introduced to Anna, Walter's official betrothed. Her brief happiness is expressed in 'Amor celeste amor.' Magda Olivero never appeared in a performance of *Loreley*. If she had, it would surely have been the title role so it seems strange to find her version of 'Amor celeste amor': needless to say, she invests it with every conceivable nuance.

At the end of the opera, Loreley, the mermaid that sailors dread, lures Walter to his death. Francesco Merli (1887–1976) joins Bianca Scacciati in what I find a thrilling recording of the finale, made in 1929. Merli enjoyed a huge worldwide career and it seems a pity not to have heard more of him during this tour of Catalani's operas. The final scena really belongs to Loreley, though. Bianca Scacciati is not perhaps the finest singer to be heard in these 78 excerpts. There is a cutting edge to her voice on records: however, by all accounts this was not so apparent during her hugely successful stage career. Be this as it may, Scacciati really is Loreley both in her earlier solo and in this final duet: Loreley indeed – listen at your peril!

Ending this survey, it is impossible to feel anything other than intense admiration for the musical skills and wonderful melodies and dramatic moments which pervade Catalani's operas. In undertaking to write this essay, I knew I had in my collection a good many 78s of his arias and duets either in original form or, in some cases, transcribed to LP or CD. I had not, though, listened to them systematically or sequentially as has been necessary during the course of writing. The cumulative impact on me is the same as with others and I am left with the feeling 'if only.' Had Catalani lived longer and given us more operas, would it have made a difference to the subsequent evolution of Italian opera? Would there have been a viable contemporary challenge to *verismo*? I have already mentioned the willingness of other collectors to allow me to listen to items not in my collection. I am grateful to them and to the authors of many books and other source materials on the great singers of the past. I am not aware of any previous attempts at analysing Catalani 78s as a whole, so this may be a first. I know of records which I was unable to hear and there are certainly others of whose existence I am unaware. And of course opinions differ. I will be only too happy to receive more information and perhaps this may in due course lead to a later edition of this essay.

He's not famous because he died young, but I've always adored Alfredo Catalani. I even named my daughter after his opera La Wally. *I was with him when he composed his piano piece,* In Sogno, *'Dreaming.' Barely a week goes by without me playing this piece: it's a way of remembering that dear spirit. He used to say: 'I wrote it, but I can't make it sound as magical as you do.' He was the most simpatico of the composers, refined – he wasn't crude as the others, Puccini, Mascagni, Giordano, or even Franchetti. He had beautiful eyes, also, and the women used to fall in love with him.*

Just before he died his skin went yellow. My mother always said: 'his eyes are always open as if he's looking into the distance.'

Toscanini in His Own Words

www.ingramcontent.com/pod-product-compliance
Lightning Source LLC
Chambersburg PA
CBHW051757040426
42446CB00007B/414